Paletitas de Guayaba

On a Train Called Absence

A Novel in Spanish By

Erlinda Gonzales-Berry

With an English Translation By
Kay (Kayla) S. García and
Erlinda Gonzales-Berry

FLORICANTO

Floricanto™ Press
650 Castro Street, 120-331
Mountain View, California 94041
(415) 552-1879
www. floricantopress. com
ISBN: 978-1-888205-20-6
La Mujer Latina Series
*"Por nuestra cultura hablarán nuestros libros. Our
books shall speak for our culture."*
   Roberto Cabello-Argandoña
   Editor

Paletitas de Guayaba

On a Train Called Absence

A Maya

Ésta es una obra de ficción. Cualquier parecido con personas reales, vivas o muertas, es producto de la casualidad.

Kay (Kayla) S. García wishes to thank the Center for the Humanities at Oregon State University for their support during the time that she worked on the translation of **Paletitas de Guayaba.**

Erlinda Gonzales-Berry is Nuevomexicana hasta las cachas. Her ancestors settled in the Río Grande Valley in 1598. She grew up in el campo in northeastern New Mexico, attended high school in El Rito, and received her Ph.D. at the University of New Mexico. In the middle of the twentieth century she moved with her family to Guadalajara, Mexico, where they lived for a year. This was a crucial formative experience for her. Gonzales-Berry currently lives in Corvallis, Oregon where she retired from the Ethnic Studies Department at Oregon State University in 2007.

Table of Contents

Paletitas de Guayaba

Erlinda Gonzales-Berry

En el tren de la ausencia
me voy
Mi boleto no tiene regreso
(canción mexicana)

Si has pensado
cambiar tu destino
recuerda un poquito
quién te hizo mujer
(canción mexicana)

MUJER CHICANA
y rompe
en éxtasis furiosa haz los
cordones de los mitos
tú sola
(Margarita Cota-Cárdenas)

El Desierto
12 de diciembre

Me prometí cuando todo terminó que no me permitiría pensar en ti, pero qué le voy a hacer. Aquí voy en un tren destartalado hacia una gran aventura que borrará para siempre el olor de tu carne y el recuerdo de tu tacto y de tu voz que aún envuelven todos mis sentidos. Mientras tanto, no me queda más remedio que fumar cigarrillos y darle vuelta a cuanta mentira, contradicción y perogrullada que se me ocurran. Así que resulta natural pensar en ti.

Qué claro diviso ahora, en este interminable viaje solitario, toda nuestra historia y empiezo a comprender cómo y por qué falló. En primer lugar, admiro la sutileza con que me tejiste un mundo de fantasías, me prometiste la luna, me aseguraste librarme de un bagaje cultural que a los veintitrés años me aplastaba con el peso de mi virginidad sofocante. Con cuánta destreza aplacaste mis temores, quitándome uno por uno los gruesos y opacos velos que me cubrían el cuerpo, desatando fibra por fibra las cuerdas tirantes que estrangulaban cada uno de mis deseos vedados. Me tomaste de la mano y me guiaste por espesos bosques de culpabilidad y de vergüenza; el más oscuro hueco de mi conciencia lo llenaste de tu luz dorada. Nuestros cuerpos son la playa, son el mar, son un vasto campo de recreo, me dijiste. Sé niña otra vez; y como niña me dejé llevar por el juego. En trance erótico, traspasé los límites banales de mi existencia restringida por años de admoniciones de fuego y de pena eterna. Como niña me entregué al placer de correr por la playa y de nadar en el mar. Qué linda eres, me dijiste; me encanta tu risa juvenil, tus brinquitos de cabrita silvestre, pero ¿ves ese puente? Hay que cruzarlo ahora porque, en fin, soy hombre y necesito una mujer. No puedo ser tu padre para siempre. Debajo de tu misma piel aceitunada yace otro mundo. Una vez más, me tomaste de la mano y me internaste en un mundo de llamas. Al principio me asusté, pero pronto vi que el fuego no era el del infierno, sino que nacía de mí misma, y cada círculo de ese incendio me produjo profundo placer. Qué linda eres, me dijiste; si te pudieras ver ahora mismo te asombrarías; tus ojos de gatita juguetona se han vuelto los ojazos de leona –¿en celo?– te pregunté yo.

Mis palabras te cayeron como plomo. Tu llama se volvió hielo, tus músculos dorados se hicieron acero azul. No puede ser, me dijiste. Tiene que ser, te contesté. Ves esa puerta. Tú me la tienes que abrir. Así como me enseñaste las fórmulas de la microeconomía, así como me revelaste el camino a la playa y al mar, me tienes que abrir la puerta a la maternidad.

Consternado e incrédulo te dijiste a ti mismo: ya me lo habían dicho. Cuidado con las niñas de tez aceitunada. En fin, te devoran. Las domina un instinto primitivo. Son capaces de brindarte los placeres más ocultos. Pero precisamente cuando te encuentras intoxicado e inmóvil ante su fulminante pasión, te entierran los colmillos en la yugular y demandan respeto, hogar y familia. Yo tan seguro de mí mismo, campeón indisputable del *pas de deux*, les contesté a mis amigos de cabellos dorados que no se preocuparan de mí. A cuántas alumnas no había introducido no sólo al mundo de la microeconomía, sino también al mundo de Eros; y al fin de su programa de estudios cada una me había colmado de muestras de efusiva gratitud, asegurándome que jamás olvidaría a su primer maestro, y una por una, había salido al mundo a hacerse la vida.

Cuidado amigo, me advirtieron. No conoces a las niñas de tez morena. No son como nosotros, que vemos la vida como una hoja de papel en blanco, sobre la cual trazamos nuestro propio destino con ojo agudo y mano segura, y después salimos a cincelar nuestras experiencias concretas según el plano proyectado de antemano. Ellas se dejan llevar por la experiencia misma, por un instinto primordial que en cierto momento les señala: ÉSTE ES. Yo creí haber creado todas las condiciones necesarias para evitar que pasara esto. No, no puede ser, me dijiste. Tú no formas parte permanente del plano que hace mucho dibujé. El jugo de tu carne no basta. No tienes tierra, no tienes nombre, no tienes familiares bien colocados. (Esto no me lo dijiste tú, sino mi misma intuición). Vete, niña de piel aceitunada y de ojos de gata, a explorar el mundo que mucho tiempo te queda para abrir esa puerta de cuya llave no soy el único dueño.

Mi error fue confundir el placer con el amor ¿verdad? Yo te quise tanto; yo te ofrecí el regalo más precioso que yo tenía para dar, y te negaste a aceptarlo. Y ahora, todo el placer que tú me diste se ha vuelto hiel y me consumen la vergüenza y la culpabilidad. Pero, sabes, aprendí algo en el proceso. Ustedes, los hombres de los cabellos dorados, se creen los dueños del mundo. Ustedes se creen Dios. A ustedes les pertenece el mundo para hacerlo y deshacerlo según su plano. Y también les pertenecen los seres humanos; a ellos también los hacen y los deshacen. Los sentimientos, las emociones ¿qué importan? Estos hay que dominarlos con un plan guiado por la razón y una visión mercantil de la vida. Así que maestro, yo no te agradezco nada; incluso te escupo la cara. (¿Te asombra mi candidez? La verdad es que dudo que tengas la sensibilidad–y perdona este profundo impulso que siento a humillarte, echándote en cara la verdad – para apreciar que la inocencia es una condición que fácilmente es reemplazada por la amargura y el rencor.)

El único consuelo que me queda es que estoy segura que algún día, cuando todo lo que te rodea te parezca desabrido, te darás cuenta de que hubo un momento en tu vida en que rechazaste la sal de la tierra.

No sé por qué me he molestado en escribir esta carta. Quizá para poner en perspectiva nuestra relación y para empezar a arreglar los pedazos de esta vasija rota desde la cual se han desparramado mis emociones y mis sentimientos como las aguas agitadas de una tormenta desencadenada por dioses furibundos. Amen.

xxx

P.D.: Por favor, no contestes. Quiero que sea mía la última palabra sobre este capítulo de mi vida.

El foco tuerto del viejo y destartalado tren penetraba la noche oscura y devoraba lenta pero definitivamente las millas vacías en su larga jornada a la ciudad macrocefálica. El traqueteo de acero sobre acero no le permitía dormir. Se sentó en la camilla, se inclinó sobre las almohadas, encendió cigarrillo tras cigarrillo, y empezó a escribir en su cuadernito:

...Dios de la vida, ¿por qué sigo con esta porquería? Lo peor es que seguramente algún día moriré de cáncer de los pulmones. Los encontrarán todos acarbonados, podridos, chamuscados, asquerosos al hacer la autopsia. Tiene razón papi. ¡Qué hábito tan cochino! Pero ni modo, mi adicción es incurable e irremediable. A lo mejor allá pueda dejarla; la reemplazaré con tequila y Tecate – y limón. ¿Por qué será que el limón siempre me recuerda mi niñez? No mi niñez allá, sino mi niñez *allá*, digo, en México. México, Jalisco, Guadalajara, la calle Simón Bolívar, los departamentos de la señora Jaramillo. Departamentos para gringos. Puros gringos, con la excepción de nosotros que también vivíamos allí, pero no éramos gringos. De cierta manera sí lo éramos, bueno no gringos (qué bárbara, cómo pensarlo), pero norteamericanos sí. ¿Cómo negar eso? Aunque habláramos español, aunque fuéramos morenitos, éramos de allá, digo del otro lado. Ni modo de cambiar eso. Y los amigos de papi, más bien los compañeros de la AFTOSA, todos güeros, y yo haciéndome la muy mexicanita, afectando la entonación del español de mis amiguitas. Y quiénes son esos gringos que van a tu casa me preguntaban, y yo que no sé, que no los conozco, que no me importa. Ustedes son de allá, ¿verdad? No. Somos de aquí. Es que mi padre tiene algunos conocidos, por su trabajo, sabes.

Y mi hermana mayor. Pinche pocha. Nomás con las tejanas asquerosas andaba. No sé por qué se metió con

ellas. Quizá por su edad no quería perder su identidad.
Era demasiado tarde para que ella se volviera mexicana.
Yo sí. Yo soñaba con nacer de nuevo, con renacer
mexicana. BORN AGAIN MEXICAN. Cuando se fueron
del colegio, sin permiso, ella y las dos gringas tejanas, yo
como que no la conocía. Oye, ¿no es tu hermana la que
viene arrastrando la Mis Beti? ¡SUÉLTENLAS! ¡QUE SE
VAYAN A CASA! (gritaba el decano por el portavoz).

Pinche pocha. Yo haciendo cola con los otros niños
de La Americana, saludando la bandera mexicana,
muriéndome de vergüenza mientras mi hermana se
largaba porque era quien era y no quería, o no podía,
renacer mexicana. Y yo muy Judas. Fíjate, que no es.
Se parece, ¿no? Pero no, no es mi hermana. Y después
vinieron por mí mis padres. No, que no te puedes quedar.
Echaron a tu hermana nomás por hablar inglés. No
podemos dejarte aquí con gente tan déspota. Te vamos a
mandar con las monjitas. Y yo prendida de la Mis Mary,
pegando gritos y llorando a baba suelta, escondida en las
enormes ubres de la Mis Mary.

And then, welcome monjitas de mi vida. Esas
señoritas sí que me hicieron la vida pesada. Yo, tan
leonina en todo, acercándome siempre al calor humano,
como las gatas, buscando al amor materno de las ubres
enormes de la Mis Mary. Qué desengaño. Aquellas
monjitas de hielo, vestidas de negro, enclaustradas
detrás de muros decorados con vidrios fatales. Las
santitas, las esposas de Cristo, las madrecitas. Qué
madrecitas ni qué madrecitas, más frías y más malas
que agua salada en la milpa (*como le dijo un perro a un
antiperro*). Así que empezaron los sufrimientos de niña
escandalosa, la mayoría de los cuales se me han borrado
de la memoria.

Desgraciadamente de los sueños no. Allí me llegan
de visita de vez en cuando las madrecitas, las cabecitas
encapuchadas, las caritas de ángel distorcionadas como
si estuvieran filtradas por un lente de ángulo ampliado.
Allí en mis sueños más privados hacen un círculo y
me empujan de mano a mano enguantada y siguen así
hasta que me caigo de cansancio llorando, y gritando

y llamando a la Mis Mary. Gracias a Dios que aquello sólo duró dos meses, porque de haber durado más me hubiera cambiado mi estatus de *born again Mexican*. La verdad es que a esas monjas las llegué a odiar, y por poco termino odiando a todo, y a toda, mexicano(a). Pero me salvé. Me sacaron de allí antes de haber renunciado a mi patria adoptiva y aquí voy de regreso, quince años después, buscando el perfume de las bugambilias, la música deleitable del español mexicano, las paletitas de guayaba, el olor del limón, el chocolate con canela, el lago de Chapala, el patio de la casa en Sayula, la calidez humana...

¿Te acuerdas, Sergio, del día que nos conocimos? Yo esperaba a Julie fuera de la librería. Empezaba a llover y me convidaste a esperar dentro. Psssss, métete para acá, te vas a mojar, me dijiste, y apenas entré me preguntaste si era chicana. ¿Cómo lo supiste? No me digas que por la manera de caminar y de vestir. Eso no es lo que opinaste aquel día; lo llevas escrito en la frente me dijiste. Y yo te contesté que sería del otro lado, pero que no era chicana, que no me gustaba esa palabra, que de donde venía yo decían que los chicanos eran una bola de comunistas, unos revoltosos oportunistas. ¿Así que no te gustan los comunistas? me preguntaste con tamaña chispa en los ojos. Entonces debes ser de Nuevo México. Según he oído decir, los neomexicanos son bien conservadores y no se sienten aliados al resto del pueblo chicano. Yo qué sé de política te dije; por el momento lo que a mí más me importa es sobrevivir en esta selva.

Cuando te conté que estudiaba en El Centro, tú, que con razón estaba tan desilusionada, que allí eran una bola de reaccionarios a quienes la única cosa que les interesaba eran los dólares de los gringos. Entonces te conté de lo mal que me iba allí; que yo había venido a México para conocer a gente mexicana, y que allí sólo había estudiantes extranjeros que casi no hablaban el español, y a mí, que lo entendía perfectamente bien y hasta lo hablaba, me habían puesto en una clase para principiantes, isque para quitarme el acento pocho. Después te conté de como cuando llegué no tenían alojamiento para mí y tuve que quedarme en casa del director y como después oí a la secretaria decir que no tenían familia para mí porque a las familias no les gustaba hospedar a estudiantes pochos. ¿Te imaginas lo que me hirió el saber que los mexicanos estiman más a los gabachos que a los chicanos? Entonces le dije a Santiago, el director, que si no me hallaba casa, iba a exigir que me devolviera mi dinero y a marcharme, y que jamás vería a otro pocho en su pinche escuela. Así fue que al día siguiente llegué a vivir con los Córdova y con Julie.

Y cuando entró Julie a la librería te dio risa y me dijiste que de algo me iba a servir mi viaje a México, que por lo menos aprendería a convivir con gringos. Qué ironía, ¿verdad? Que allí no nos aguantamos y aquí me tocó compartir recámara con una güera. Eso sí, no hay como vivir con el objeto de nuestro prejuicio para comprender que es nuestra humanidad lo que nos une a todos (y algún elemento perverso de esa humanidad lo que nos separa).

Oye, dile a Carlos que si trata a Julie como un estropajo viejo, yo misma lo mato. Qué chistoso, ¿no? Toda la vida he odiado a las güeras y aquí estoy defendiendo a una. La verdad es que Julie es bien padre, pero pobrecita, no la dejan estar en paz un momento tus compatriotas. Espero que Carlos no sea como otros chavos que ven en Julie una cogida gratis y se acabó, porque Julie no es así. Sí, ya me contaste eso de la mentalidad colonizada de los mexicanos y como después de tantos siglos de dominación han asimilado la mentalidad de esclavo, codiciando la propiedad del dueño porque es su única manera de vengarse de él. Los mexicanos ni empiezan a entender los motivos de su comportamiento, pero allí andan hechos bobos persiguiendo a cuanta rubia pisa tierra sagrada, seguiste con toda seriedad. Y yo: nunca lo había visto así; creía que lo hacían nomás para probar que son machos. Cómo ibas a verlo así, si no te gusta la política. Mira, ¿cómo te llamas? Marina, nuestras vidas son la política, me dijiste, y si no lo son, lo deben ser, y tú debes ser chicana; es tu responsabilidad moral conocer el movimiento chicano. Entonces sacaste el montón de artículos y el libro de Acuña y me dijiste que lo leyera y que después veríamos si era o si no era chicana. Me prometiste también presentarme a tus amigos chicanos de Casa Aztlán.

Durante toda la semana no hice más que leer. Abandoné las clases en el Centro y hasta se me olvidó la rabia que se había apoderado de mí cuando empecé a sentir el rechazo de los mexicanos hacia sus hermanos del otro lado. Claro, cada día empiezo a entender mejor ese resentimiento que sienten hacia los que se van en busca del dorado proverbial. Es que son tan profundas las heridas que sienten ante su historia, nuestra historia, que es natural que odien a los que se van para allá.

¿Sabes lo que quisiera hacer, Sergio? Quisiera hacer una encuesta sobre las actitudes de los mexicanos hacia los chicanos. ¿Qué te parece? Podría incluir cosas sobre aspectos culturales, políticos, lingüísticos, fuentes de información, etc. Lo que verdaderamente me interesa es eso de las actitudes hacia nuestro español porque me exaspero tanto con los mexicanos. No sé por qué no pueden darnos crédito por algo. Hace más de un siglo que vivimos bajo la bandera norteamericana donde el inglés es la lengua dominante y de prestigio y donde se ha hecho todo lo posible por erradicar el español. Pero a pesar de eso nos aferramos a él, aunque sea machacado, como dicen aquí. Lo importante es que lo sentimos nuestro y lo conservamos con orgullo. Lo que no entienden aquí, es que el español es una lengua estigmatizada en Estados Unidos porque la gente que lo habla es estigmatizada, de segunda categoría. Menosprecian nuestra cultura y nuestra lengua; nos tratan como animales—

NO DOGS
NEGROS
MEXICANS

decía un rótulo en los restaurantes y las albercas en el sudoeste en los cuarenta y cincuenta – pero no nos exterminan del todo, no nos echan en los hornos, porque necesitan de nuestros brazos, de nuestra mano de obra barata. Tenemos que esforzarnos en aprender el inglés porque sólo así nos podremos defender, y claro, nuestro español va a sufrir en el proceso, pero no por eso lo vamos a abandonar. Aunque se hayan negado a enseñárnoslo

en las escuelas, aunque seamos un pueblo analfabeto
en la lengua que mamamos en la leche, lo seguimos
reclamando como nuestra lengua natal e insistiendo en
nuestro derecho a hablarlo a pesar de que el inglés es la
lengua oficial del país. Y todo lo que pueden decir tus
compatriotas es que qué bárbaros los pochos, mejor ni
lo hablaran del todo.

    ¿Entiendes lo que te digo? ¿Cómo que calle por
un rato? Ay, Sergio, ¿no ves cuán importante es para
mí hablar de todo esto? Pero, eso sí, de coger nunca te
cansas, ¿verdad? Quien les bautizó a ustedes de Latin
Lobers bien sabía de lo que hablaba. No, no es que quiera
reducirte a un estereotipo – te lo digo para que se te
infle el ego, bueno y eso también. Claro que me gusta;
cómo no me va a gustar si sabes tan perfectamente bien
cómo complacerme. Mmmmmmmm. Allí. No. No. Más
arriba. Allí...Perfecto. No, no tan fuerte.... Ahora sí, sí,
sí, Sergio. Ay mi amor, mi vida, ¿de quién más voy a ser
si no tuya? Si quieres probarlo, mátame. ¡SÍ, MÁTAME
PERO NO ME DEJES! (claro, en voz exageradamente
beltranesca).

    ¿Cómo que qué escandalosa? ¿Y loquita también?
Bueno, eso sí, bien zafada, como diría mi mamá (ay, y qué
diría si me viera ahora, ¡qué horror!). Loca por ti y loca
de amor, igual que tú, ¿verdad? Bueno si no loco de amor
por lo menos debes admitir que bien lelo de deseo carnal,
porque si no lo estuvieras, ya me hubieras dicho que
me largara a la porra y te dejara en paz porque ya estás
hasta el colmo de mis rollos. Pero sí entiendes, ¿verdad,
Sergio? esta necesidad obsesiva que tengo de darle voz
a mis frustraciones, a mis dudas, a mis sueños y a mis
rabias, en fin, de ordenar mi mundo y de comunicarme
con alguien que me entienda, y ese alguien eres tú, mi
querido Sergio.

...Pues ¿qué hago? La escribo o no la escribo. Ya la tengo formada palabrita por palabrita aquí en la mente. Pero qué saco con escribirle. Eso ya terminó. Que se vaya mucho a la fregada, a la tiznada y hasta la mismita chingada si se siente inclinado. A mí me importa un pito. Yo nomás le dije chaucito baby, y se acabó, fini, caput-o. Ay, y a quién se me hace que engaño? Aquí llevo el corazón sangrando en las manos, y sigo tratando de convencerme de que no me importa. Pero, ¿qué pasó? No entiendo. Le di todo lo que yo tenía para dar y me rechazó. Ahora lo que más deseo es comunicarme con él, escribirle para crear un puente de palabras que se estire a través de esta nada espacial que nos separa. ¿Cuántas millas serán ahora? ¿Quinientas, setecientas? ¿Qué más da? Con cada una de ellas se hacen más agudas su imagen y su presencia. A ver, podría decirle algo así: *Aquí voy en una aventura que borrará para siempre el olor de tu carne y el recuerdo de tu tacto y de tu voz que aún envuelven mis sentidos....*

Sergio, no sabes, cuando tardaste en llegar, el temor que me dio. Sí, yo sé que ya estás aquí. Pero eso de nada me sirve cuando te vas de la ciudad. Yo sé que no me vas a contestar, pero te voy a preguntar lo mismo de siempre. ¿A dónde fuiste? ¿Qué hiciste? ¿Cómo que no puedes? No me tienes confianza, ¿verdad? No, no quiero reñir. A ver, quítate la camisa y te doy un masaje.

Sí, toda la tarde la pasé en Casa Aztlán. Estuvimos hablando un largo rato Isaura y yo. Sabes, me cae retebién. ¿Te acuerdas que al principio le tenía miedo? Cuando me acostaba era difícil dormirme porque a cada rato creía que se metía en mi cama. Y sabes, ahora me da vergüenza porque me doy cuenta de que ese miedo me acusaba de haber asimilado prejuicios que muy poco distan de los pusilánimes prejuicios raciales que tanto odio. En fin, el miedo al prójimo no es otra cosa sino una de las múltiples caras del prejuicio, ¿no te parece?

Pues, sí, yo lo supe desde el primer día que me llevaste a Casa Aztlán. ¿No te acuerdas de la pelea de almohadas que tuvimos? Tú crees, mi bienvenida a Casa Aztlán fue un bombardeo de almohadas. Casi me morí de risa y de cansancio, pero en ese momento de frivolidad descabellada supe que estaba con familia. Antes de que me llevaras con ellos me sentía tan desilusionada, tan derrotada que quería regresar a Nuevo México. Pero cuando los conocí a ellos, a Toña, a Manuel, a Beto (qué cabrón puede ser Beto, ¿verdad?), a Lupe, a Luis y a Isaura, todo cambió.

¿Te acuerdas cómo comenzó la pelea de almohadas? Jamás se me olvidará lo que dijo Isaura después de la rozadita que me di con Beto, quien al momento de entrar empezó a picarme y a insultarme porque soy manita. Es que los manitos, los pocos que he conocido, siempre me han caído gordos. Por su orgullo, ¿sabes? Se creen muy gachupines y no quieren unirse a la causa, porque isque no son chicanos. Y tú inmediatamente pusiste cara de ándale Beto, les dije que esta nena necesita cariño y ternura y ya tú empiezas con tus necedades. ¿Qué le dije yo entonces? Tienes razón, mi vida, me puse a explicarle que yo me sentía mexicana porque había vivido aquí cuando era niña pero que en ese momento me sentía muy desengañada porque el rechazo de los mexicanos había sido tan abierto y tan despiadado. Fue entonces cuando dijo Luis que ni se lo contara, que todo eso ya era parte de la experiencia colectiva de todos los que vivían en Casa Aztlán. ¿Por qué crees que estábamos aquí juntos? Porque vivir aquí es igual que vivir en un barrio o en una colonia chicana en Estados Unidos; Casa Aztlán nos protege del mundo hostil que se encuentra allí fuera. No, no fue Toña sino Lupe la que intervino: bueno, es verdad, uno se siente así al principio, pero a medida que se va acostumbrando y se va mejorando el español, va perdiendo uno el miedo y poco a poco se abre uno entrada y ya se le hace menos hostil el ambiente, especialmente en la UNAM, porque, ideológicamente allí tienen que aceptarnos.

¿Es verdad, Sergio, que es tu ideología lo que te impulsa a preocuparte de mí? Yo más bien quería que fuera tu biología, tu cerebro reptiliano. Sabes que he formado una nueva hipótesis sobre el por qué los turistas se portan como tontitos inmorales al llegar a México. ¿Quieres oírla? Bueno, pero primero tienes que inspirarme. Pues, ¿qué sé yo? A ver qué te inventas. ¡Uuuuuuuy, chavo de mi vida, a eso habría que llamarle inspiración divina!

Bueno, aquí te va. Es que allá todo es tan estéril, tan blanqueado, tan artificial que se ha entumecido la porción reptil del cerebro, digo, así, como en forma de evolución colectiva. Sí, todos son iguales. Ahora bien, cuando vienen aquí (bueno, venimos, porque yours truly también ha experimentado el fenómeno, hasta cierto punto) los colores, los olores, los ruidos de la calle, las miradas que penetran hasta el alma y que sólo los mexicanos saben dar, bueno en fin toda esa sobrecarga

de estímulos extraordinarios que nos llegan por los
sentidos, despierta la colita del reptil y nos volvemos
loquitos bailando sobre la mesa, pegando gritos de
charro, tomando pulque hasta permanecer paralizados,
acompañando a desconocidos a hoteluchos de quinta,
en fin, comportándonos como si no hubiera mañana,
ni infierno tampoco. Es un momento de desequilibrio
mental, digamos, que ocurre al encontrarse uno en un
mundo tan vigente y tan distinto al suyo.

¿Entiendes? Así es, amorcito corazón, que estos
deliciosos momentos que pasamos juntos se los debes
a los mangos maduros del mercado que despertaron
mis apetitos carnales, encapsulados en un pequeño
lagartijo que antes dormitaba aquí, mira, aquí mismito
en la base del cráneo, pero que al despertar se ha vuelto
un enorme cocodrilo devorador de jóvenes esbeltos y
prodigiosamente dotados. A ver, repite lo que acabas
de decir. A ver si verdaderamente dijiste lo que creo
que dijiste. Que no sabes por qué tu lagartijo no se
encuentra en la base de tu cráneo sino entre tus piernas.
¡Ay, qué ingrato! Me paso toda la semana esperándote
para contarte lo que se le ocurrió a mi cerebro de pollo,
y lo mejor que tú puedes hacer es salirme con esa
pendejada. Pero qué más hay que esperar de buen niño
conscientizado y comprometido. ¿Tú dime? Bueno, esta
vez te perdono, y si te sosiegas un rato, sigo con lo de
Isaura.

Lo de Isaura. A ver, ¿dónde iba? Ah sí, Beto, pinche
Beto a quien le dio por provocarme, *sans cause juste*.
Oyes manita, volvamos a eso de considerarte chicana.
Yo como que no te creo, ¿sabes? Según mi experiencia
la ideología atrasada de los manitos es impenetrable,
incontrovertible y asquerosa. Así lo dijo, ¿verdad? Y
entonces dije todas esas cosas maravillosas de ti. ¿Te
acuerdas? A ver, empecé así: újule mano, primero tengo
que probarles a los mexicanos que soy persona de valor;
ahora tú me demandas lo mismo. No sé qué habría hecho
yo aquí si no hubiera conocido a Sergio. Es la única
persona que no me ha tratado como basura. Por sus ojos
(sí, por *teus olhos belos, meu bem*) voy descubriendo y

comprendiendo las profundas laceraciones que afligen a este país y a su gente. A través de él voy entendiendo los motivos del rechazo que hacia nosotros muestran los mexicanos, pero aun más importante, a través de él voy entendiendo la historia de mi pueblo, y eso es lo más irónico; tuve que venir a México y conocer a Sergio para conocer el movimiento chicano.

De todos modos, siguió insistiendo el mancebo de la lengua afilada. ¿Cómo que la mía no es tan embotada? Apenas le dije que se dejara de joder y sugerí que a lo mejor la razón por la cual seguía picándome era porque fue una manita la que le dijo que era un imbécil que nomás no...y no pude terminar porque intervino Toña. Mari, no te agüites. Es que Beto siente tan apasionadamente todo esto de la causa chicana que a veces se le pasa la lengua. Pero, créeme, tiene cosas verdaderamente alumbradoras que decirnos a todos respecto a nuestra identidad, nuestra historia, y las soluciones que precisamente en este momento se nos ofrecen a la raza.

No, no. Lo que le dije fue: ah, pues entonces hay que perdonarle su descortesía. A ver, cuéntame Beto. No hay cosa que me complazca más en todo el mundo que oír a un cretino pontificar perogrulladas. Fue ENTONCES que dijo Isaura – por fin llego a lo de Isaura: Ven Mari, te enseño nuestra recámara. Después pueden hacer las paces tú y Beto. Ahora nos toca a nosotras, las bellas damas de Casa Aztlán, darte algunos consejos referentes a cómo sobrevivir en esta jungla urbana, rebosante de machos mexicanos, la presente compañía excluída (tan ancho tú), y de una pequeña banda de vatos locos chicanos que cualquier día de la semana les podrían dar lecciones a los nativos en cómo insultar, ofender, y reducir al segundo sexo a mera carne cruda.

Me pareció muy bien dicho y también me encantó la porra de Toña: HIT EM AGAIN, HIT EM AGAIN, HARDER, HARDER, pero fue lo que contestó Beto lo que me dejó boquiabierta: újule, Sergio si le tenías designios amorosos a la manita, olvídate, porque ya la trae Isaura con su perorata lesbiana. Pues, después de oír eso, mano, empecé a sentirle miedo. Pero ahora que la conozco he descubierto que es humana – y verdaderamente creo que los heterosexuales tendemos a ver a los que no lo son como una especie subhumana – y la aprecio profundamente porque cada día me hago más consciente de la triple discriminación que contra ella opera. Claro, que esa conciencia templa un poco mi rabia personal.

Ya te dije que allí es donde me mordió el perro, cuando le metí un popote en la oreja. Papi se puso tan furioso que quería matarlo, pero mami no lo dejó. Mimada, tu abuela, Sergio, porque a mí jamás me mimaron mis padres. Incluso, ¿sabes lo que dijo mami? Que yo no era más que una malcriada, pleitista que siempre andaba fastidiando a pobre Otelo – te lo juro así se llamaba el perro. Tú crees, mi misma madre defendió a un can, a un *chien*, y a mí me mandó a la quinta fregada. ¿Cómo que no voy a sufrir complejos freudianos? Tú dime, amor. Cinco años. Claro que me dolió. Pues bésala si quieres, pero la verdad es que no me duele. Y esa cicatriz que tienes tú en la espalda, ¿qué te pasó? ¡Que alguna tarde muy larga cuando tengas muchas ganas de hablar me lo contarás? Uj, ya lo veo. Yo, una ancianita de 80 años: dígame, don Sergio, ¿qué le pasó allí donde tiene esa cicatriz en la espalda? (Risas y carcajadas desmesuradas).

Pues, sabes que fue ese día en Casa Aztlán que me enamoré de ti. Espera, déjame ordenarlo. Fue cuando lanzó Beto su insulto a Isaura que ella y Toña empezaron a tirarles almohadas a los muchachos. Después se armaron ellos y empezaron a volar proyectiles emplumados por todos lados. Entramos todos menos tú que te quedaste en la butaca nomás viéndonos. ¿Cómo que viste aquello como una celebración exclusiva de chicanos? ¿Verdad? ¿Como una especie de rito de iniciación para mí? Qué chistoso, a mí nunca se me ocurrió eso. Bueno, de todas maneras, cuando caímos todos apilonados se apoderó de mí un sentimiento de ambivalencia verdaderamente extraordinario; por un lado quería permanecer allí, absorbiendo la intimidad que me ofrecían mis nuevos amigos, bueno en realidad mi nueva familia, y por otro, cuando miré hacia donde tú estabas, allí solito y marginado (no hay duda alguna, mi

gran debilidad son los chavos solitarios y melancólicos),
sentí ganas de abrazarte, de besarte los párpados, los
bellos y prominentes pómulos (vestigio de antiguas
razas autóctonas me dije) y los delgados y finos labios
detrás de los cuales yacían deseos inarticulados que
se volvían sustancia al escapar por tus ojos y dirigirse
impávidos hacia mí. Sí, en ese preciso momento en que
me sentí unida a mis amigos chicanos, sentí también el
 deseo de acostarme contigo. Creo que así soy, que ésa
es mi naturaleza. En el momento exacto en que estoy
por identificarme total e irreductiblemente con algo,
una parte mía se detiene y huye en dirección opuesta.
Claro que se presta a cierta, bueno no esquizofrenia
propiamente dicho, pero a neurosis sí, desde luego.

Y allí lo tienes. Esa fue la tarde que me enamoré de
ti, y para probártelo voy a ofrecerte, ahora mismito, el
regalo más anhelado por los varones de todos los rincones
del mundo:

*¡Oh, éxtasis! Visita a este buenmozo y hazle esclavo
de este hábil instrumento sin el cual sería imposible
levantar calumnias contra el prójimo, confesar
flaquezas y pecados, cantar corridos, decir aaaaah bajo
órdenes del médico o saborear paletitas de guayaba...*

...Ay Dios, ¿cómo puede vivir esta gente en este desierto de mierda? Arena y más arena, una que otra casuchita devorada por vientos voraces. Dios de la vida, ¿qué comen? Esta tierra no rinde ni siquiera un bocado. No se alcanza a ver ni un sólo pueblito en este vacío infinito. Sin embargo siguen apareciendo, como fantasmas, caminando al lado de la vía. ¿Hacia dónde? Aquí no hay nada. Es la nada absoluta. Es la soledad pristina. Este espacio jamás fue designado para sostener la vida humana. Pero allí va ese señor con su bestia, sus siluetas negras de relieve contra el cielo enllamarado del amanecer. ¿Cuál será la diferencia? Tú dime, Dios. Tú que creaste a ese hombre a tu imagen, y a esa bestia, y este hoyo vacío y este majestuoso amanecer, ¿Cuál es la diferencia entre la vida de ese hombre y la de su bestia?

No te sentí entrar. Es que estaba durmiendo y soñando. Espera, me está volviendo. Mi abuela, sí, estaba soñando con mi abuelita. Me estaba haciendo un traje, una blusa de encaje y una falda amarilla, como cuando era niña y vivía con ella. Siempre me hacía vestidos. Desbarataba los suyos y los cambiaba y los hacía a mi medida. Entonces me decía, anda mídetelo. Cuando me veía con el nuevo traje se le encendía la cara de placer. Ven, déjame peinarte. Luego me peinaba y me ponía maquillaje. Nunca tuvo hijos. Es que era mi tía abuela, no mi abuela. Era tía de mi papá pero como no tuvo hijos, le pidió a su hermana – sí la que se casó con su primo– que lo mandara a vivir con ella y siempre fue como su mamá. Así que por el lado de papi tuvimos dos abuelas, una abuela, y la otra, tía abuela a quien llamábamos abuela. Cuando yo tenía diez años le pidió a papi que me dejara vivir con ella porque mi abuelo trabajaba en un rancho y sólo venía al pueblo los fines de semana y ella se ponía muy triste. Así que me fui a vivir con ella. Al principio fue muy raro. Yo estaba acostumbrada a mis hermanas y la bulla y el desorden que siempre había en casa. Con mi abuela todo siempre estaba arregladito y se hablaba en voz baja. En casa todas siempre hablábamos a la misma vez, y gritábamos y chillábamos y siempre era un carnaval. Donde mi abuela todo era distinto.

Después de vestirme y peinarme me decía que si no quería ir a visitar a mi mamá porque ella tenía dolor de cabeza y quería dormir un rato. Así que me iba yo feliz de la vida con guantecitos y con una cartera de cuentas de colores que era de ella. Al llegar a la casa de mis padres, mis hermanas siempre estaban con los quehaceres de la casa, lavando platos, limpiando el piso, planchando, barriendo el patio. Entraba yo, muy princesita y me miraban con cara de ay qué asco y apenas me hablaban. Yo iba a hablar con mamá y las podía oír cuchicheando y riéndose de mí. Antes de irme, me arrinconaban y empezaban a pellizcarme y a jalarme el pelo. Cuando llegaba donde mi abuela yo ya venía toda desgreñada y con el traje nuevo roto. Y cada vez que podía, regresaba con ilusiones de que esta vez me tratarían bien y jugarían conmigo, pero ni modo. Siempre era igual. Después de unos años volví a vivir con mis padres y todo eso se olvidó y volví a integrarme a la familia. Creo que esa experiencia tuvo un efecto muy profundo en la formación de mi personalidad. En primer lugar, siempre la usé como motivo para manipular a mis padres. Les salía con que ustedes no me querían y me regalaron a la abuelita como a cualquier huerfanita. No, la verdad es que yo estaba tan feliz de estar una vez más donde había señas de vida que muy pronto los perdoné. A veces nos acordamos y me llaman la princesita y yo las llamo las cenicientas y nos da mucha risa.

Pues mi abuelita murió el año pasado. Ay Sergio, fue la cosa más horrible y deshumanizante que jamás podrías imaginar. Después de hacerle una operación la conectaron a un montón de máquinas. Estuvo así durante diez días con tubitos en la boca, en la nariz y por donde quiera. La piel la tenía amarilla y llena de moretones. Nunca abrió los ojos y nunca supimos si estaba consciente o no, y las malditas máquinas forzándola a respirar. Mami y papi se pusieron muy mal, pues ya te puedes imaginar viéndola así. Papi peor porque a él le había quedado la decisión de sí o no hacerle la operación. Si no se la hubieran hecho, habría muerto a las pocas horas, pero al hacérsela siguió viviendo en ese infierno mecánico y claro, él se sentía culpable.

Conocimos a otra familia; bueno, mi hermana ya la conocía porque eran de su pueblito. Un hijo de dieciocho años había chocado en su moto en frente de la casa de sus padres el día de su graduación de la secundaria, y también estaba como verdura conectado a las máquinas. Era una familia enorme de diez hijos, y esposos, y niños y los viejitos. Pues esos diez días los pasaron en el hospital. Arreglaban camas en el piso del corredor y allí dormían. Traían comida y en fin, vivían en el corredor.

Cada hora, permitían entrar a uno o dos familiares a ver a su paciente. Los dos, el joven y mi abuelita estaban en condiciones iguales. No se movían, no hablaban, no abrían los ojos. Nomás se oía el siseo de la máquina respiradora. Y a cada hora del día y de la noche entraba alguien a verlos así por tres, cinco o diez minutos. Los que entraban se quedaban allí de pie mirándolos sin saber qué hacer. Papi por fin ya no aguantó y se rehusó a entrar a verla porque le causaba tanta agonía. Así que nos turnábamos las hermanas y mamá.

La décima noche entré con mi hermana, la que hace tiempo se metió a una religión aleluya o qué sé yo. No me lo vas a creer pero cada aspecto de su vida está ligado a su religión. Lo peor es que verdaderamente cree que las mujeres deben obedecer a sus esposos sin el menor reparo porque así lo manda la Biblia. Bueno, antes de entrar habíamos estado hablando y todas habíamos quedado de acuerdo en que era absurdo que la tuvieran viva a pura fuerza de las máquinas. Que lo que merecía era morir con dignidad en su casita. Los médicos, olvídate, que es nuestra responsabilidad moral tenerla así mientras sigan funcionando tres órganos vitales y que quién sabe cuántas más pendejadas nos decían.

Pues esa noche eran como las once cuando entramos a darle vuelta como lo habíamos hecho durante diez días. Como era la primera vez que entraba con Luz, me quedé sorprendida cuando empezó a hablarle. Las demás de la familia no decían nada; nomás se quedaban allí mirándola y llorando y todo lo demás. Pero Luz de una vez se puso a hablarle como si nada. Le decía que Dios la esperaba con los brazos abiertos, que ya era tiempo que le diera su alma, que no se resistiera a su voluntad, que el cielo era bellísimo, que había jardines y huertas por todos lados, que el abuelito la esperaba en el cielo y no sé cuánto más. Y la abuelita seguía como siempre, inerte, sin dar señas de oír o de comprender nada. Pero, sabes, de pronto empezó a ocurrir la cosa más rara. A medida que mi hermana le hablaba, acariciándole siempre la frente, empezaron a cambiar los números en la máquina que le registraba el pulso. Cuando entramos estaba a 140.

Poco a poco empezó a bajar: 135-134-133-130. A medida que le bajaba el pulso a mí se me aceleraba y se me hacía difícil respirar. Pues, fíjate que jamás había visto a nadie morir y se me hacía que allí a mi ladito estaba la calaca, tú sabes, personificada, tamaña risa y todo eso. Cuando por fin marcó 94 la máquina, se detuvo, pero seguía el siseo de la respiradora. Pronto entró la enfermera a decirnos que era tiempo de salir. Salimos al corredor, Luz, la misma estampa de la serenidad, yo totalmente histérica. Ella me abrazó e inmediatamente sentí una ola de calma extenderse a través de mi cuerpo. Así estábamos abrazadas cuando salió la enfermera a decirnos que había muerto la abuelita.

La escena que presencié esa noche me dejó verdaderamente impresionada. Y todavía todo ese episodio de la muerte de la abuelita – el horror de las máquinas, la frustración de verla así ni viva ni muerta durante tanto tiempo – me obsesiona y me agobia. A veces logro olvidarlo por algún tiempo, pero hoy volví a recordar. Quizá quiera que rece por ella y por eso la soñé. Es lo que dicen cuando uno sueña a los muertos, ¿no?

¿El muchacho de la moto? Murió esa misma noche, a las doce.

Mire, tráigame una rebanada de papaya, una taza de café con leche y unos molletes. Eso es todo. No, espere un momento. ¿Tienen cigarrillos? Los que sean, con tal de que ardan, que produzcan humo y cáncer y que no tenga que esperar hasta la próxima parada. Tiene razón. Así me dice mi papá. Pero qué le voy a hacer, soy adicta incurable.

....Y usted, viejo verde, ¿qué mira? A poco su señora no tiene piernas. Uuuj, ni senos tampoco. Pobrecita. Y de este lado otro. Por lo menos éste se limpia la baba con la servilleta. Y su señora quizá está ciega. Si yo fuera ella le daría una bofetada: Toma cochino, bobo descarado, deja de empelotar a esa muchacha y cómete tu desayuno....

No. No necesito nada. Verdad que no. ¿Cuánto falta? ¿Dice que hay parada en Durango? No. Me siento bien. Es que voy muy cansada. Anoche no dormí.

....Cómo friegan estos camareros. Nomás porque vengo de allá se les hace que me acuesto con ellos como cualquier gabacha. Creo que por eso no dormí anoche. De puro miedo que se metiera uno a mi alcoba. Pero en realidad, en el fondo no siento miedo. No como allá donde te ultrajan en media calle, a plena luz del día y todos mirando como bobos. Pero papi y mamá me contaron no sé cuántas cosas horripilantes de cómo son los mexicanos. Como si fueran distintos a nosotros. Creo que lo que pasa es que allá nos han inculcado la idea que somos superiores a ellos. Especialmente en Nuevo México, a la raza no le gusta que le llamen *Mexican*. I'm not *Mexican*, I'm Spanish te dicen de una vez. Yo les digo a mamá y a papi, pero ¿no ven que somos de las mismas raíces, que somos hermanos? ¿A poco somos distintos porque nos separa una frontera abstracta, unos trapitos de colores? Ésas son ideas que nos han metido los americanos (con mis padres no se permite usar la palabra gringo). No, hija. Ellos son surumatos. Son gente violenta y desconfiada. Vienen aquí y nos quitan los trabajos (not to mention las güisas a los chavos). Ni modo.

Así piensan mis padres y muchos más como ellos. Gracias a Dios que no tengo esos complejos. A México yo lo defiendo como mi misma patria. En efecto lo es. La patria que adopté cuando niña. Por eso regreso ahora. Para reclamar mi paraíso perdido. Mis padres no sienten el amor que yo siento hacia México. No hay que culparlos a ellos, puesto que nacieron allá. Sus padres también nacieron en territorio norteamericano y sus abuelos también, no porque quisieron, sino porque ése fue el momento histórico que les tocó vivir. Estoy segura sin embargo de que las generaciones anteriores sintieron algo por México. A pesar de que no nacieron en lo que políticamente se define como México, estoy segura que lo llevaban en la subconciencia colectiva y que les latía en las venas. La prueba está en que en nuestra lengua, en español, siempre nos hemos llamado mexicanos. Lo de *Spanish* es cosa del inglés – para caerle bien al AMERICANO. Hasta maromas le hacemos si creemos agradarle. Qué pendejos, mano. Porque la verdad es que nada de lo que hacemos les agrada. El gran mito de allá es que quieren aceptarnos, que quieren brindarnos la preciosa igualdad democrática norteamericana. Jes sir, con tal de que nos transformemos en su misma imagen, que olvidemos el español, que nos rindamos a su modo de ser.

Qué ilusión. ¿Cuándo nos daremos cuenta de que jamás nos aceptarán como iguales? Y no es sólo por cuestión de la piel morenita. Es cuestión de la labor de burro. Si nos aceptaran como iguales en las universidades, en las profesiones, si prepararan bien a nuestros hijos en las escuelas estatales, ¿quién haría la labor de burro? ¿Quién piscaría las cosechas, quién trabajaría las minas, quién trabajaría en las maquiladoras, quién en las enlatadoras, quién pavimentaría las calles, quién lavaría los platos sucios, quién limpiaría los retretes, los servicios, los inodoros, los excusados, los comunes? ¿Quién?...

...Con cuánta destreza aplacaste mis temores, quitándome uno por uno los gruesos y opacos velos que me cubrían el cuerpo. ¡Ay, criaturas desamparadas! ¿Cómo es su vida en ese jacal de zoquete? ¿Dónde juegan? ¿Qué toman para el desayuno? ¿Saben de dónde viene y a dónde va este tren, o termina su mundo en el horizonte blanco del desierto?...

Cuando hice los apuntes en un cuadernito, la verdad es que no tenía ninguna intención de que todo aquello llegara a formar un texto. Los hice, en primer lugar, porque me parecía que era lo que había que hacer uno al emprender un viaje – cualquier viaje que durase más de doce horas. Después, muchos años después, en una tarde nublada, una de esas que inspiran el trajinar en los escombros del pasado, descubrí el cuadernito. Al leerlo, me sentí feliz de haber recuperado algo de mi pasado que ya casi había olvidado. También sentí una leve diversión al descubrir que hubo un momento en que había sido tan ingenua. Los apuntes sobre el viaje concreto, o sea, sobre el traslado espacial por tren desde la frontera al D.F., abrieron las puertas a la memoria.

Empezaron a fluir imágenes y voces que no sé cuánto hace las había reprimido. Durante varios días no pude hacer más que recordar. Lo que más me sorprendió fue que el recuerdo de él, de ninguna manera lo habían alterado los años, la madurez, la experiencia, o lo que fuera lo que meditaba entre el presente y aquel pasado hasta hace poco olvidado. El recuerdo venía envuelto en matices apasionados y arrebatos románticos, digo, el recuerdo porque después de haber llegado al D.F. había abandonado el intento de documentar mis "aventuras" en el cuadernito. De él no existía ni siquiera un apunte. Sólo quedaba la memoria. Y una carta.

No sabré decir exactamente cuándo me dio por juntarlo todo, digo los apuntes del viaje y las memorias de postviaje en un texto. Creo que la culpa habría que echársela a los apuntes. Aunque ingénuos, como dije antes, me parecía que revelaban cierta, qué sé yo, actitud interrogativa que quizá podría interesar a quiénes se afanan actualmente en descubrir la voz femenina (ni qué decir de la voz femenina chicana) que hasta hace poco había permanecido oculta tras las voces canonizadas de la cultura occidental. (Nada modesta, dirán ustedes. La verdad es que la modestia la fui perdiendo con los años y con los regalos que nos trae la vida).

Una vez decidida a escribir el texto, me pareció lógico empezar desde el principio y proceder en forma cronológica hasta el fin, aunque debo admitir que no estaba segura de a cuál fin me refería, pero sentía la certidumbre de que dicho fin se presentaría a su debido tiempo. Como ya se habrán dado cuenta, no resultó así el asunto. A medida que iba escribiendo a máquina (y redactando, inventando (?) los apuntes, los cuales me parecían de alguna manera auténticos y objetivos precisamente por ser apuntes, se me aferraban los recuerdos no-apuntados y, por lo tanto, menos empíricos pero no menos insistentes. Casi sin darme cuenta empecé a mezclar los apuntes con los recuerdos (y *¿qué de las fantasías?*). Resulta supérfluo decirles a ustedes que todo se volvió carnaval, o sea, un enmarañamiento de pasado y presente y futuro. Durante varios días me molestó la pérdida de lógica temporal, pero al fin resolví que lo que iba a ser la segunda parte (había proyectado dividir el texto en dos partes: 1) la ida y 2) la estancia; lo de la vuelta no me interesaba del todo puesto que había regresado rápidamente por avión engrifada hasta las orejas y poco o nada recuerdo de ella), también era parte del viaje, si no en el sentido geográfico-espacial, ciertamente en el sentido espiritual. Pero de eso ustedes ya habrán intuído lo obvio.

Perdóname, amor, que llego tarde. ¿Te dije que íbamos a reunirnos con Dolores Huerta quien anda aquí en un intercambio con varios sindicatos? Pues Beto hizo los arreglos. Tú sabías que él había trabajado con Chávez cuando empezaron a organizar en California, ¿verdad? Pues Beto quería que la conociéramos y quedamos en vernos con ella en el Sanborns. Tenía una cita en Los Pinos a las 9:00 y al salir de allí, ya sabes, lo de siempre; hubo un embotellamiento y la tuvimos que esperar hasta las 12:30. Pero, créeme, valió la pena. Es verdaderamente una persona extraordinaria. Nos habló con tanta paciencia de sus actividades con el sindicato y de sus sueños para los campesinos. Además se interesó en nosotros; nos preguntó qué hacíamos aquí, cómo la pasábamos, y nos convidó a trabajar con la UFW al regresar a los Estados. Pues, a lo mejor sí lo haga cuando regrese. No sé, Sergio. Por el momento prefiero no pensar en eso, pero algún día tendré que regresar, ¿no es cierto?

La verdad es que quedé muy impresionada con ella. Es una persona sencilla, pero dinámica y sobre todo genuina. Sabes que tiene siete hijos pero eso no le impide ser una de las líderes más activas del sindicato. Nos impresionó a todos. Queríamos que pasara a Casa Aztlán a comer con nosotros, pero ya te puedes imaginar su itinerario. Después de despedirnos de ella, pues como que no podíamos separarnos. Sentíamos algo así como si hubiéramos estado con una profeta. Nos sentimos espiritualmente elevados y quisimos hablar un rato, prolongar la sensación colectiva de inspiración. Pues la conversación terminó como siempre, con un largo y animado discurso de Beto. Ya sabes cómo le encanta instruirnos como si fuéramos sus discípulos. Bueno, en cierto sentido lo somos. Por él vamos analizando y ordenando todo lo que leemos, lo que estudiamos en la

UNAM y en los círculos, relacionándolo todo a nuestra realidad, tratando de llegar a una mayor comprensión del proceso histórico que cinceló la experiencia chicana (perdóname el cliché, pero a veces es tan difícil expresarse uno de una manera original).

Fíjate que ya nos llevamos mucho mejor. La verdad es que lo respeto mucho y aprecio la dedicación y el cariño (aunque a veces le cueste expresarlo en actos simbólicos) con que nos guía. Aun Isaura, a quien saca de quicio a veces su fachada machista, lo respeta. Creo que poco a poco está cediendo su actitud patriarcal y que ha aprendido tanto de nosotras como nosotras de él, porque créeme, no desistimos un momento en nuestro plan de sensibilizarlo. Me parece que por fin se va dando cuenta de lo absurdo que resulta hablar de la opresión si no se le abre camino en la lucha a la mujer. Como ustedes en su organización, ¿hay mujeres, verdad? Y participan plenamente, ¿verdad? Es que toma tanto tiempo borrar esos gruesos estratos de lavado de seso cultural. Pero es posible. Difícil, pero posible.

Bueno después de despedirme de ellos, me vine en el camión y me puse a pensar y a tratar de darle forma, o quizá nombre, qué sé yo, a las experiencias que he tenido desde haber llegado a México. Como ya sabes, yo vine aquí por motivos puramente egoístas. Deseaba recobrar mi pasado personal; venía en plan – en cierto sentido espiritual – pero también en plan de aventura. Había terminado mis estudios en la universidad y era tiempo de pasar al mundo del trabajo y la responsabilidad, pero sentía la necesidad de pasar primero por alguna especie de rito. Además, desde haber ingresado en la universidad, a donde llegaban muy pocos de nosotros, y los que sí llegaban tendían a sufrir una metamorfosis desaculturizante, yo sentía que con cada nueva interacción social se reducía una parte muy esencial de mi ser. O sea, que las aguas de la asimilación me iban arrastrando río abajo como a la pobre Serpentina. Había por allí clamores de algo –Chávez, Tijerina– pero nuestras familias nos advertían que todo eso nada tenía que ver con nuestras vidas. Afortunadamente no fue posible huir de ello. Aquí estoy, quién lo hubiera pensado, descubriendo el movimiento chicano en México. Pero a veces se me hace que todo es un poco artificial, que debo regresar para verdaderamente aprovechar el estudio en un contexto práctico. Es decir, lo que me hace falta es vivir este fenómeno de tan amplia envergadura.

Venía pensando también que nosotros, los chicanos, representamos una especie de síntesis y de sincretismo. Allá estamos tan constantemente conscientes de nuestra posición marginada, de nuestra relación defensiva con ese espacio que nos es extraño, y por lo tanto caótico, que nos vemos forzados a mantenernos en un estado de tensión constante con esa otredad. Nos sentimos permanentemente amenazados; a cada paso anticipamos que alguien nos meta traba, ya sea literal o figurativamente. Es este constante estado de alerta lo que he bautizado la neurosis chicana —en realidad la neurosis, o sea, la doble conciencia, que aflige a todo ser marginado— y fíjate que no utilizo el término en su sentido negativo porque es precisamente esta neurosis, este estado exaltado de autoconciencia lo que nos impulsa a afirmarnos y a superar los obstáculos de esa sociedad que nos rechaza. A esa otredad amenazante le ofrecemos en forma de contrafuerza nuestro mito de mexicanidad. Nos aferramos en nuestras fiestas mexicanas, en nuestra música, en nuestra quinceañeras, y en símbolos como la Virgen de Guadalupe, símbolos que aun tú me has dicho van perdiendo significado en el México contemporáneo; y ahora con el movimiento chicano, suscitamos nuevos símbolos, algunos de ellos rescatados de los escombros de momentos que quizá para ustedes ya hayan perdido su vigencia.

Yo sé, por ejemplo, que a ustedes se les hace chistoso que reclamemos mitos precolombinos para alimentar nuestra ideología naciente. Sin embargo, ustedes mismos conjuraron esos mitos en una etapa no muy alejada de su historia, y no lo pueden negar porque eso sería negar a Rivera y a Orozco, a Paz y a Fuentes. Pero todo ese artificio cultural, por lo anacrónico que les pueda parecer a ustedes, es una etapa necesaria en nuestro camino

hacia la autodeterminación. Hay que nutrirnos de algo
y esos mitos y esos símbolos nos hacen fuertes porque
nos permiten rescatar nuestra historia. Además son
nuestros amuletos contra ese demonio que nos rechaza
a la vez que amenaza devorarnos. Pero luego venimos
aquí, y de pronto es obvio que no somos mexicanos. Nos
sentimos desorientados porque la otredad aquí –claro
menos hostil– resulta ser precisamente lo que allá nos
sirve de amparo. Y justamente aquí está lo más raro:
hay ocasiones en que me siento inclinada a ofrecer mi
"sajonidad" como reacción a la enajenación que aquí
me envuelve.

Pero mira, creo que por fin, después de sufrir
innumerables penas y dolores psíquicos –y muy
consciente estoy de que todo es relativo puesto que mis
aflicciones pasan por peditos mudos en la escala universal
de convulsiones humanas sísmicas– me doy cuenta de
que no somos ni anglos ni mexicanos. Ocupamos un
espacio particular en el continuo que corre entre esos
dos polos. Ese espacio que ocupamos se caracteriza
en la superficie por matices de los respectivos polos
diametrales. No obstante, en su estructura profunda,
se encuentra algo nuevo. Creo que llegará un momento
en que ya no nos sintamos obligados a ofrecer nuestra
mexicanidad, sino nuestra chicanidad como respuesta
a nuestras circunstancias. Esto es, afirmar nuestra
neurosis chicana, igual que les expone Leopoldo Zea
a los latinoamericanos afirmar su barbarie y utilizarla
como marco teórico para definir el mundo occidental,
o sea, aquella realidad extranjera que quiso despreciar
lo americano al aludir a ellos como la barbarie. Me
parece que son nociones análogas, el chichanismo y la
barbarie; en ambos casos se vuelve positivo y motivo
de autodefinición lo que en otra ocasión fue negativo y
denigrante.

Tienes razón, vida, el peligro sería quedarnos
enmarañados para siempre en esa falsa seguridad
de unicidad cultural o en soluciones culturales a un
problema universal porque eso sólo nos separaría de
las masas marginadas del globo. Bien entiendo que

el análisis que acabo de proponer tiene sus límites; sin embargo creo que es un paso imprescindible en el sendero hacia la liberación. Un pueblo oprimido (ay, qué vacía suena esa palabra, ¿verdad? ¿qué haremos para restituirle su significado?) tiene que saber quién es y cuál ha sido su historia para saberse parte de todos los pueblos oprimidos.

Y no creas que no me doy cuenta que entre palabra y la acción existe un gran trecho. Tú, por ejemplo, eres modelo de quien ha reconciliado esos dos aspectos del compromiso. Pero es mucho más difícil allá, ¿entiendes? Quizá porque vivimos en una opulencia tan desmesurada, y porque nuestro sistema ha manipulado el racismo con tanta destreza como para evitar la conjunción y la colaboración de los varios grupos marginados, el habla es barata y la acción mínima. Ahora mismo, lo que ocurre allá es algo insólito y no dudaría que dentro de unos años la cooptación haya borrado todo menos la memoria.

Y para cambiar un poco de tema, puesto que veo que tus bellos ojos tienen sueño, Sergio de mi vida, tú crees que no sé nada, pero sí sé que fuiste a Guerrero este fin de semana, y también sé que algo les salió mal porque te veo decaído, y cada día veo tus ojos más tristes. Ay, Sergio, abrázame, tenme cerca. No sabes cuánto temo que te pase algo. Por favor, ámame, Sergio, ámame.

Se habrán preguntado más de una vez por qué es que no le he dado ni voz ni corporeidad a él. De eso no estoy totalmente segura. No obstante, les ofrezco algunas posibilidades que se me ocurren a medida que voy poniendo los dedos en las teclas: 1) la técnica la vi en la novela de un escritor mexicano y me dejó muy impresionada; 2) no lo recuerdo bien, o lo recuerdo muy bien pero es tan dulce el dolor de ese recuerdo que no quiero compartirlo; 3) él realmente es el/la lector/a con quien desea Mari entrar en una íntima relación; 4) habrá entre ustedes quienes dirán que él nunca existió, que no es otra cosa que la proyección de su/mi/nuestra visión particular del varón ideal, o sea, el Segundo Sexo inventando al Primero tal como quisiera que fuera.

*Mi error fue confundir el placer con el amor,
¿verdad? Yo te quise tanto; te ofrecí el regalo más
precioso que yo tenía para dar, y te negaste a aceptarlo.*
Mira, Mari, es absurdo lo que tú propones. Yo jamás
he pensado en el matrimonio. Me gusta mi vida tal
como es y no siento ninguna necesidad de cambiarla.
Además tú eres demasiado joven. El abrumarte con las
responsabilidades del matrimonio, y peor aún, de una
cría sería destruir tu juventud. Si quieres, podemos
seguir como estamos. Eso me agradaría mucho. Pero si
no puedes aceptar esas condiciones, haz lo que tengas
que hacer. Algún día comprenderás que lo que hago es
por tu bien. ¿Y quién eres tú para decirme lo que a mí
me conviene? Lo que aquí ocurre es que eres demasiado
egoísta para aceptar la responsabilidad. Tú sólo quieres
divertirte sin compromiso y eso me parece el colmo.
Además, ¿no es hora de estrenar otra virgencita? Ya te
conozco tus manías y harto difícil sería convencerme que
no es uno de los placeres de tu vida el iniciar a neófitas.

    Mari, no digas tonterías. Yo sé que todo esto te duele,
pero créeme, el matrimonio sería un desastre para los
dos...

Erlinda Gonzales-Berry

Qué rico, Sergio, estar contigo otra vez. Pues te diré la verdad, la playa estuvo divina, pero la especie humana que allí se encuentra, olvídate. En primer lugar, cuando llegamos, claro, totalmente aterrorizadas puesto que fue nuestro primer viaje largo en camión, no encontramos taxi que nos llevara al hotel. Por fin, se nos acercó un chavo, de unos veinte años, diría yo, y nos dijo que él nos llevaría. Le preguntamos si era taxista puesto que no llevaba la lucecita esa en el coche y dijo que sí, que su compañía estaba de huelga, pero que él seguía dando jalones clandestinamente –eso, clandestinamente– porque tenía que hacerse la vida. Tú dime, ¿qué íbamos a hacer? Allí estábamos superlistas para pachanguear y abandonadas en la estación de camiones.

Pues regateamos un rato y por fin aceptamos. Al subirnos al coche vi que iba manejando otro chico, así todo golfo con su chaquetita de cuero, y el pelo teñido, pues no exactamente rubio sino más bien anaranjado y bien tostadita la piel. Ándale, tipo beachboy. Nos subimos las cuatro, Toña, Lupe, Julie y yo en el asiento de atrás y el otro chavo adelante. Pues yo ya iba con mis temorcitos de siempre, ¿sabes? pero no dije nada. Y el golfito que no le quitaba los ojos –por el espejo– a Julie. Pues para empezar, no arrancó el coche; allí nomás nos quedamos estacionados un rato. Y yo que qué pasa. Es que allí enfrente está estacionado un jefe de la compañía y no queremos que nos vea, y el golfito mirando intensamente a Julie por el espejo. Por fin hizo arrancar el coche pero no caminamos a ningún lugar. De pronto vi que el golfito les hacía así a los focos, off-on-off-on, tú sabes, como si estuviera señalándole a alguien.

Pues más vívida que película en tecni, se me presenta en la mente, así como un flash rápido, una escena a la Macon County Line. ¿A poco esas películas no les llegaron? Menos mal, no les hace falta ese tipo de porquería. Lo que vi fue una playa desierta, como que ni siquiera una gaviota, tres coches atacaditos de golfos circundando el "taxi," y el golfito pelirrojo aún pelándole el ojo a Julie, saca un enorme machete a la vez que escupe entre los dientes, allí las tienen cuates, a todas menos a la güerita; ésa me toca a mí. Y eso fue todo, pero bastó para que se me subiera la presión. Empecé a sudar la gota gorda. Cuando ya no aguanté, perdón me siento mareada; tengo que salir. Tan cortés como si fuera verdadero caballero, me abrió la puerta y me dejó salir el otro chavo. Fui directamente hacia un policía que andaba por allí. Me miró así incrédulo cuando le dije, pues mire, es que esos chicos ofrecieron llevarnos al hotel pero no sé si son o si no son taxistas porque se están comportando muy raro. Creo que están contemplando raptarnos y después ultrajarnos. Usted, ¿qué sugiere que hagamos? Toña, mientras tanto, cuando me vio ir hacia el policía, pues también se asustó, y sacó su navajita –isque es para pelar frutas y nunca sale sin ella– por si acaso. Por fin salió el chota de su trance de y-a-esta-loca-qué-le-picó y le señaló a un taxista que acababa de estacionarse en frente de la estación. Ándale, Chemo lleva a estas pochas a su hotel, y ustedes señoritas ya no se anden subiendo con extranjeros (como si Chemito fuera amigazo de toda la vida).

Pues allí vamos hechas peor que sardinas, esta vez en un Volkswagen y el taxista más amable que vendedor de coches usados. Cuando por fin llegamos al Faro me preguntó Lupe que qué había pasado en la estación. Cuando les conté lo de mi premonición, pues se atacaron de risa y empezaron a vituperarme con sus ¡ay Mari, tú siempre tan histriónica! Ya no eres niña. ¿Cómo nos vamos a divertir si tú vas a andar friquiada (tú sabes, desquiciada en dialecto chicano) y con tus temores y tus pendejadas? Qué ingratas, ¿verdad? Yo acababa de salvarles la vida y ésas fueron las gracias que me dieron. Gracias las del payaso, como diría mi mamá. Pero en fin les dije, bueno, de ahora en adelante no digo nada; simplemente las sigo a ustedes y a ver hasta dónde llegamos. Right on, Mari y no sé cuanto pedo. Pues ya verás, vida, los líos en que me metieron esas amiguitas isque liberadas.

Mira, acomódate. Dame esa almohada. Pon las piernas aquí. ¿Quieres un frajo? Pásame tu encendedor. No, eso no, tontito. Okay, baby. STORYTIME.

Después de descansar un rato, salimos a la playa. Allí estábamos absorbiendo vitamina D cuando se acercaron unos alemanes. Empezamos a maderearnos con ellos, que de dónde eran, que qué hacían en Mexicles y todo eso, ¿no? Claro que no les dijimos que éramos del otro lado; les dijimos que éramos del D.F. Cuando ya se había puesto el sol nos convidaron a ir a tomar una copa y después a cenar, pero que primero tenían que pasar por su hotel por dinero.

Cuando llegamos al hotel, inmediatamente me dejé caer en una poltrona en el lobby. Hacía un calorazo del infierno afuera. De una vez empezó el que se llamaba Hans con que subiéramos, darlinks, con ellos. Que tenían buen tequila y Noche Buena. Al oír la marca mágica, salté de la silla y todos nos encaminamos hacia el ascensor. Pues nos sirvieron y estuvimos allí charlando un rato. No, sí se les entendía bien. Con muchas eses ápicoalveolares, con la zeta castellana y con la elle lateral palatal. Así mira: [eṣpaŋa], [θapato], [kaʎe]. En fin muy madrileño su español. Nosotras muy impresionadas porque tenían un suite con dos recámaras, dos baños, sala y cocinita, todo muy arregladito, pues ya sabes cómo son los alemanes.

Ya yo iba en mi segunda copa de tequila cuando pasó Hans a la recámara y salió con una maleta. La abrió, sacó una cámara y un pequeño televisor. Cuando acabó de armar todo el juego me di cuenta que era una cámara de video y allí mismo empezamos a salir en la pantallita de la tele. Lupe de una vez se entusiasmó –ya sabes cómo le gusta estar ante la cámara siendo bailarina y todo. Bueno Toña es un poco tímida y hacía lo posible por esconderse, y Julie cool as a cucumber como nomás ella. Tan fresca como un pepino. No, Sergio, no creo que sea alusión sexual, es simplemente una expresión sin sentido. Empezaron todos a jugar con la cámara, claro menos yo. No sé por qué, pero empecé a sentirme

un poco incómoda y le dije a Julie: I smell a rat. Me oyó
Lupe y no tardó en proclamar ¡ay Mari, deja de hacer
escándalos! En eso dice uno de los chicos, creo que se
llamaba Peter, ¿no creen que hace demasiado calor aquí?
y se quitó la playera quedando en traje de baño y, créeme,
amor, esos alemanes llevan lo que se llama bikini. Fíjate
que no tienen vergüenza. Pues así dicen, que siempre
son ellos los primeros en encuerarse en la Costa del Sol.
Pues, Lupe, que por allí debe tener algún abuelo alemán,
siguió el ejemplo y también se quitó la playera y la falda
que se había puesto sobre el traje de baño.

Entonces saltó Hans a la cámara y empezó a enfocar
sobre Lupe y a gritar *kommt mal, zieht euch aus, kleine
Häschen* que según Peter quiere decir anden conejitas,
quítense la ropa. A mí todo esto me cayó gordo.
Llámale intuición o sencillamente sentido común, pero
justamente cuando dije, yo me voy al hotel, salió Erik
de la otra recámara con una P38 Walther. Es que Steve
tenía una. ¿No te he contado lo de Steve? Yo creía que sí.
Bueno una de estas tardes te cuento. Entonces dijo Erik
miren muchachos lo que me compré en el mercado esta
tarde. En el mercado, ¿tú crees? ¿Les gusta? y me miró
a mí al decirlo. I got the message, babe. Volví a sentarme
y me quité la playera simulando haber entrado en el
jueguito que estaba a punto de volverse un poco grotesco.
Mis compañeras, pues olvídate, como si anduvieran
hipnotizadas. ¡No se daban cuenta de nada! Allí andaban
bailando como si jamás hubieran conocido la inhibición,
y el maldito ojo de la cámara siguiéndolas. Yo viéndolas
en la pantalla, anticipando, horrorizada por dentro, la
escena escandalosa que estaba por desarrollarse, y Erik
jugando con su Walther, acariciándola y a cada rato
mirando hacia mí.

De pronto di con un plan. Salté de la silla y me quité la
falda. Claro que traía mi traje de baño, el bikini que tanto
te gusta. Corrí y abracé a Hans y empecé a darle besitos en
la oreja. Nada retrasado el mensito. Vamos a la recámara.
Vamos le dije. ¿Llevamos la cámara? En un rato, le
dije. A mí me gusta un warm-up primero. Se rió y me
guió hacia la puerta. Nadie se dio cuenta que habíamos

salido. Al entrar en la recámara la recorrí rápidamente con los ojos. Cuando me agaché para desenlazarme las sandalias, me arrebató del brazo derecho el bruto, me lo torció detrás de la espalda y me tiró sobre la cama. Hans, si quieres ser tigre, primero tienes que ser gatito. Con calma le dije. Mira, tú nomás acuéstate aquí y déjame abrirte la puerta a placeres jamás imaginados en climas nórdicos. Nosotras las mexicanas conocemos los secretos eróticos de los aztecas. Secretos pasados a seres escogidos por Coyolxauqui. Secretos practicados únicamente por vírgenes entrenadas sobre los guerreros prisioneros en víspera de su sacrificio. Abrió unos ojazos Hans y dijo ¡Oh darlink, soy tu prisionero!

Del ropero saqué dos camisas, las desgarré, lo amarré a la cama y lo amordacé, pero no antes de haber quitado las sábanas. De la sala oí a alguien gritar en voz amenazante "te dije que te lo quitaras." Eso fue lo que me dio coraje para hacer lo que sabía que tenía que hacer. Rápidamente junté las dos sábanas con un nudo, y la orilla de una la até a la cama. Abrí la ventana; me mareé al mirar hacia la tierra, pero sin más ni más me dejé ir del octavo piso. Nunca me pregunté a dónde pensaba llegar. Afortunadamente, la sábana llegaba justamente al balcón del suite inmediatamente debajo del de los alemanes. Cuando oí unos gritos de señoras bien educadas supe que había gente en el balcón. Pero muchacha, dijo uno de los señores, hay mejores maneras de suicidarte. Escuchen por favor, necesito ayuda. Rápidamente les expliqué que mis amigas estaban en peligro.

Después supe que el señor que fue a la puerta de los alemanes y anunció con máxima autoridad que la señorita Lupe Quiñones tenía una llamada de emergencia en el lobby, era un general del ejército peruano que andaba de vacaciones en Acapulco. Después nos sacaron él y su señora a cenar. Oh sí, las chavas. Pues salieron así muy ordenaditas como si nada, poniéndose las playeras y despidiéndose de los alemanes, hasta luego muchachos, chaucito, gracias por todo. Los alemanes se quedaron en la puerta con la boca abierta y de los ojos les salía fuego. Al despedir al general en el séptimo piso, empezamos a reír a carcajadas y así salimos del hotel y seguimos a lo largo de la calle hasta llegar al Faro. Y a cada rato decían las muchachas, ay Mari, loquita y escandalosa Mari, nos salvaste de las pezuñas del demonio. Pues me imagino que lo hallarían atado a la cama ¿no? Bueno después tuvimos algunas experiencias más placenteras. Como te dije, salimos a cenar con el general, y olvidando nuestro plan original de buscar chavos, decidimos gozar de nuestra compañía femenina. En fin, nuestro primer viaje a Sin City México tuvo sus buenos momentos. Pero sabes algo, Sergio, te extrañé un montón. Incluso hablamos mucho de ti. Les extraña tanto a mis amigas que yo pueda ir a donde quiera, que salga con otras personas si me da la gana, que te cuente todo y que sigamos queriéndonos loca y apasionadamente. Les cuesta mucho creer que no te pones celoso, que no te portas como si yo fuera tu propiedad privada. Siempre terminan diciendo, Sergio no es el chavo típico. En fin, es un tipo que verdaderamente cree en la libertad y que vive su ideología. Es verdad, Sergio; eres muy especial.

Y ahora, darlink, soy yo prisionera tuya, así que realiza sobre mi persona tus deseos más ocultos.

Señorita. Aguascalientes. Si quiere puede bajar un rato. Pero no se vaya lejos. No la queremos dejar, güerita. Por favor no me llame güerita. ¿No ve que soy como usted, más prieta que noche sin luna? Pochita entonces. ¿Le puedo llamar pochita?

...Cabrón, llámame lo que te dé la gana porque ya me imagino lo que me llamas en tu mente. Tetona, culito lindo. Esas palabritas, mano, las llevas impresas en los ojos. ¿De veras crees que me gusta que me desvistas con los ojos a la vez que te acaricias instintivamente los cuates? ¿Verdad que tenía razón mi amiga con su diálogo imaginario que inventó cuando viajó por México en camión. ¿Todo bien señor? ¿Negativo el autoexamen de cáncer de los testículos? ¿Verdaderamente crees que me gusta? Hijo, qué retrasado mental; qué poco sabes de las mujeres. Qué mitos se han inventado ustedes los Latin Lobers para mantener sujetas a sus mujeres. El mandamiento décimoprimero de la sagrada y varonil iglesia católica mediterránea (y curiosamente el único que se afirma positivamente): 11). Cosifíquenlas; así se asegurarán el reino de la tierra. Las cosas nada pueden contra el derecho y el poder masculino...

Es verdad Sergio, prometí contarte lo de Steve. Pero sabes que ahora me parece tan alejado y tan frívolo aquello, que ya no tiene chiste. Tienes razón, es parte de mi pasado y, por lo tanto, sería absurdo negarlo. A ver, habría que empezar con lo que recuerdo –ah, sí, el dolor.

Hubo un momento en que me sentí tan ofendida y tan herida que me parecía imposible recuperarme. Ahora veo que ésa fue la reacción de un ego débil e inmaduro. Mira, yo era joven; había tenido muy pocas relaciones con muchachos porque mis padres siempre fueron estrictos conmigo. Y de aventuras sexuales, olvídate. El puro temor a la confesión me había mantenido en estrictas condiciones de virginidad. Pero con Steve todo pasó de la manera más natural. El era mayor que yo –cosa ya un poco fuera de lo ordinario puesto que allí los jóvenes tienden a mezclarse sólo con personas de su edad. Al principio todo fue una hermosa aventura, pero a medida que nuestra relación se fue desarrollando, me ocurrió algo raro. Empecé a sentirme sobrecogida por algo –como te diría– algo casi primordial que me hizo querer tener una hija, o un hijo, lo que fuera, con él, y empecé a insistir en el matrimonio. Ahora que lo pienso bien, veo que fue una astucia de mi subconciencia, una cortina de humo levantada para ocultar el verdadero motivo, o quizá debería decir los verdaderos motivos, porque nada es tan fácil como para tener un sólo motivo, ¿verdad?

Generalmente son los hombres quienes proyectan a la mujer como objeto para así empeñarse en ser su dueño, pero en este caso, fui yo la que empezó a sentir *una imperiosa e implacable necesidad a relacionarlo todo al amor que de noche viene*, y después confundí el amor con el derecho a poseer. Me hice creer que el matrimonio, ese marco estructural impuesto por motivos económicos, costumbres sociales, y decretos legales, me otorgaría el derecho exclusivo a poseerlo. Aunque no sabría elucidarte las causas tras mi actitud, podríamos especular que se debía sencillamente a mi inmadurez y al hecho de que fue mi primera aventura amorosa. Agreguemos a esto el hecho de que en la misma leche mamé los inspirantes ejemplos de los cuentos de hadas y los tuve siempre como modelos a seguir. De niña, cuántas noches no le supliqué a mi mamá, linda mami, que me abriera las puertas al sueño y al ensueño con las bellas imágenes de La Cenicienta, y cuántas veces, creyendo que me hacía el gran favor, accedió, articulando, cual suaves ondas de clavicordio, palabra por palabra mi cuento favorito. ¿No ves que desde niña soñé con el día en que llegara mi gallardo y guapo príncipe, me metiera el piecito delicado en la chinelita de vidrio, y me llevara a vivir en su castillo en las nubes? En este caso habría que reemplazar la chinelita de vidrio con un diafragma de hule, pero en fin, apareció mi anhelado príncipe. Como no nos fuimos inmediatamente a vivir allí por las nubes, muy pronto empecé a sentirme culpable por haber entrado en una relación ilícita. (Qué absurdo, ¿verdad? hablar así de una relación entre dos personas que se quieren).

Había veces en que me ponía a pensar en qué sería de mí si él me abandonara. Me empezó a obsesionar un profundo temor que nació de este razonamiento: ya que había probado los frutos vedados, y me habían caído retebién, ¿cómo le haría para evitar el seguir cayendo en el pecado de la carne con otros hombres si él me dejara? Después de darle no sé cuántas vueltas a esta noción absurda, resolví que mi única salvación estribaba en el matrimonio, estado que me concedería la respetabilidad y me vedaría la vereda a la promiscuidad. Él, claro, se negó a acceder a mis súplicas y rompimos la relación. En sus palabras: ningún favor me haría al casarse conmigo; además, algún día me daría cuenta y le agradecería el favor que sí me hacía. Yo, claro, quedé destruída. Ay, Sergio, qué chistoso; isque lo eché a rodar por mi actitud imperialista y mi neurosis católica. Sólo a ti se te ocurriría decirlo así, pero en fin, es verdad.

Fue un poco antes de venirme para acá. Sabes, cuando venía en el tren le escribí una carta muy amarga, echándole a él toda la culpa. Más que nada fue una manifestación de venganza. Pero sabes, en estos últimos meses que he pasado contigo, creo que he aprendido algo importante, o sea, que no se puede poseer a un ser humano. Aunque sea natural querer pasar todas las horas del día con quien uno ama, es tan importante que cada uno de la pareja guarde su independencia. Al no hacerlo, se destruyen. Ay, eso, hazme el favor. No, ya no lo veo como pecado ni de la carne ni de la nada. Creo que por fin me he deshecho de mi bagaje cultural y de mi socialización genérica. Este cuerpo es mío y seré yo quien decida qué hacer con él. Cuando quiera tener una hija lo haré porque es lo que verdaderamente quiero hacer, no porque quiero atrapar a un hombre. Y, fíjate, no es que crea necesariamente en la intimidad gratuita e irresponsable, sino que sencillamente he desmitificado esos decretos sociales designados para mantener a la mujer en casa, preñada y con la pata rota, y al hombre trabajando como burro para sostenerla. Lo increíble de todo este proceso es que lo haya sobrevivido sin un montón de complejos patológicos. Por qué será, Sergio, que la cosa más natural de la vida, se hace tan compleja. ¿Manipulación de la propaganda capitalista, dices? Te concedo toda razón. Sólo hay que oír los anuncios comerciales para ver eso. Es un verdadero milagro que no haya más mancos sexuales en este mundo. ¿No te parece?

A ver, ahora cuéntame tú de algún rito de pasaje personal. Podrías titularlo: *From Adolescence to Maturity: The Adventures of a Young Latin Lober*. Ya lo sé, eres hombre de pocas palabras y prefieres la acción a la palabra. Pues, me ofrezco sin resistencia alguna y, a ver, darlink, cuáles secretos me revelas hoy.

*Vamos a hacer algo que jamás hayamos **feito**, le dice la joven e inocente Hemingway a Woody Allen.*

Paleeeetaas. Tenemos de fresas, tenemos de plátano, de limón, de guayaba. Cómprese una paletiiiitaaaa...

...¿Me compro una? For old times sake? Una de fresas, guayaba. Whatever you do, don't drink the water and don't eat them street popsicles. They're made from sewer water and they'll give you such a case of Montezuma's revenge you'll just shit yourself to death. ¿Qué venganza de Moctezuma ni que la chin! Initiation rights: iniciación escatológica al tercer mundo. Devolver el sistema a su estado natural ecológico. Devolverle todos los bichitos a ese sistema lavado, blanqueado, esterilizado. ¿Para qué posponer lo inevitable? Pero en el tren no. Mejor espero hasta llegar al D.F. Entonces me como diez paletitas y me inicio sin titubeos. Have no fear, Pepto Bismol is here. Oye, qué metida de pata la de nuestro ex-jefe de gobierno nacional la vez que vino a México a visitar al otro Jefe Máximo y en pleno público, ante las cámaras de la tele, anunció que le encantaba México a pesar de que Moctezuma se quería vengar del Tío Sam a través de él. Qué bien aquel anuncio donde aparece un tipo mexicano, así todo Latin Lober, en frente de un hotel neorquino y dice —en español no less— en la tele de gringolandia: Vine de viaje a Nueva York y me dio un caso increíble de diarrea. Gracias a Dios que traje mi Pepto. Dos puntos para escritor de anuncio comercial número 390.568. Así que ¿qué decido? To shit or not to shit. On the train, that is the question. Chale, mejor espero.

So you mean to tell me that you spent the entire break in Aguascalientes thinking about excrement and Pepto Bismol? I can't believe it. You're sick.....

Ándale güerita, digo pochita, ya nos vamos. ¿Qué te pareció Aguastibias?

...¡Ay! Cómo has cambiado. Ya me hablas de tú. Todavía nos queda una noche de viaje y te haces ilusiones de que esta noche sí la haces de Latin Lober en mi camarín. ¿Verdad? Cara de metate (ésta para ti, Denise

Paletitas de Guayaba 57

Chávez), pendejo, machón mexicón (creo que así más o
menos lo dijo José Agustín).

Dios de la vida, no sé por qué vengo así, hecha
perra, buscándole pleito a todo mundo. Estos pobres
muchachos qué pueden hacer. Son productos de su
ambiente. Si son machos es porque sus circunstancias
se lo demandan. No sé por qué me encabrito porque son
tan obvios en la manifestación de sus apetitos carnales.
La verdad es que no hay gran diferencia entre los latinos
y los gabachos. Todos aspiran a la misma cosa, pero
aquéllos son más sutiles. Todo eso de que me interesas
como persona, me importa mucho lo que piensas, lo que
opinas, tu visión del mundo, es pura trampa. En fin los
objetivos son iguales, sólo los métodos son diferentes.
After all is said and done, todo lo que les interesa es
encontrarse un hoyito húmedo donde reposar (cómo que
reposar, más bien escribir *agitar*) su infame y precaria
masculinidad. (Ándale, no te hagas la delicada; no me
andas con eufemismos; dale nombre a ese instrumento
sagrado, vehículo y portador del ego masculino, el verbo
hecho carne, extensión obscena, motivo de nuestro
pavor, objeto de nuestro deseo, la cosa del hombre, la
picha, la chora, la verga, la manguera, la tripa, la estaca,
la pinga, la moronga, la herramienta, la cara de papa,
la trompeta, la menina, el pájaro, el pollo, el palo, el
chichote, el chile, el chorizo, el bicho, el pepino, el pipote,
el pitito. ¿No ves lo mejor que se siente una al haberla-lo
llamado por sus nombres? ¿Verdad que el nombrar las
cosas es encontrarle un hilito a la libertad?

Qué jueguitos se hacen ustedes (¿ustedes?), bueno,
nosotras, las mujeres –que esa palabra no la debo decir,
que esas cosas no las puedo hacer, que te dejo tocarme,
pero nomás poquito, aquí y aquí, porque me estoy
guardando para mi esposo y porque no quiero que pienses
que soy puta. Lo que necesitan, bueno necesitamos hacer,
es preguntarnos si nos gusta o si no nos gusta. Y si acaso
contestamos que sí, admitirlo, afirmarlo, pero, por Dios,
acabar con los juegos. Porque de no hacerlo, van a seguir
controlando nuestros cuerpos y nuestras vidas para
siempre, los hombres, los curas, nuestras madres –a

pesar de sí mismas. Sí, admitirlo y gritarlo en voz alta, ME GUSTA Y LO HAGO SIMPLEMENTE PORQUE ME GUSTA y no porque es mi obligación conyugal, o porque quieres un hijo, o porque soy puta. Sencillamente decir: lo hago porque me gusta y me da la gana. Al cura qué le importa. ¿Cuánto tiempo hace que llegué a esa conclusión y que dejé de confesarme porque ya no aguantaba ese rito insípido y represivo: Bless me father for I have sinned...I petted three times. Above or below the waist? Once above and twice below. Over or under your clothes? Once over his clothes, once over and once under mine. Y dejar de confesarme ¿qué resolvió? A poco el día después salí y le ofrecí mi joyita al primer macho que vi. Demasiado arraigada llevamos esa represión que nos carcome y nos niega nuestra humanidad como para deshacernos de ella como si nada fuera. ¿Cómo será ser güera? ¿Ser libre de esos complejos inculcados por nuestra religión y por nuestra cultura patriarcal? Ese recelo que les sentimos, que les siento yo a las güeras, no es otra cosa que el disfraz de mi temor, temor a mi carne, temor a mi feminidad, temor a mi esencia. Mierda, ¿dónde están esos malditos cigarrillos?

¿Sabes algo? No te (me) entiendo; primero te quejas de los hombres y de las güeras por ser tan agresivos, luego abogas por la sexualidad sin rienda para todas las mujeres. Bueno, mira, lo de las güeras se debe sencillamente a la cochina envidia. No ves que toda la vida se nos ha dicho que la belleza sólo viene en paquetitos rubios y altos. Pues nosotras –que por qué negarlo, también venimos siendo víctimas de la vanidad y del lavado de seso que nos inculca la noción que somos objetos sexuales– nos fregamos porque ya sabes eso de que las condiciones climácticas en los hemisferios del sur sólo producen lo chaparro y lo moreno. Bueno, lo rubio con una botella de peróxido se arregla, ¿verdad? Pero tú dime cómo estirar el cuerpo. No nenita, el único remedio que nos queda es aceptar nuestra condición y pasarnos la vida reteacomplejadas porque no somos la rubia que todos quieren. Y para acabarla de fregar, a su belleza le podemos agregar la libertad y la soltura que su cultura les ofrece. Así que si me quejo de las güeras allí lo tienes; mi actitud no es otra cosa que un profundo resentimiento impulsado por una insidua manipulación sicológica que nos inmoviliza y nos niega el derecho a nuestra potencia humana.

Y en cuanto a los hombres, es que me da no sé cuánta rabia que abusen de las mujeres. Pero creo que su actitud se vuelve abusiva, y fíjate que hablo solamente del ámbito sexual, no de las miles de otras facetas de la opresión de la mujer por el hombre −que quizá vengan siendo la misma cosa− precisamente porque las mujeres no han, no hemos, aceptado nuestra sexualidad. La reprimimos y nos inventamos no sé cuántos jueguitos, afanándonos en esperar al macho, en negar nuestros deseos, en hacer siempre el papel de víctima. Así nos absolvemos de los que nos han hecho creer ser pecado, ya que la víctima ¿qué culpa tiene? (Y bien sabes que el eje, el principio fundamental sobre el cual se basa y se nutre nuestra cultura es la culpabilidad). Mientras tanto, el hombre se ve forzado a ser el agresor, a rondar el balcón, a acechar a su víctima, y así se van desarrollando las sutilezas, y las no tan sutilezas, de lo que debería ser acto íntimo, humano y libertador, pero que en realidad ha sido distorcionado y deshumanizado por reglas sociales designadas a mantener a cada quien en su lugar: allí los niños, inventando y creando el mundo; las meninas aquí, cultivando las condiciones óptimas para la gestación y el desarrollo del genio creador masculino. ¡Újule, nena! ¿No te da dolor de cabeza de tan profundo y serio pensar?...

Otra vez fue un evento turbulento que nos llevó a la orilla del abismo donde una subcorriente atávica y primordial aniquiló toda conciencia de unicidad, nuestros estigmas genéricos, el signo positivo y el negativo, inexorablemente imanados, depositados en las aguas oníricas de un lago cósmico, donde nadamos sin esfuerzo en un espeso líquido uterino. Yo me veía en otra época, en otro lugar, nadando en las mismas aguas, primero en la escalera de una cantina de esas de olor a madera oscura que forman el centro vital de toda villa europea con un hombre rudo, un campesino borracho que me rogaba que dejara mi trabajo de mesera y me fuera a vivir con él en su choza de piedra, construída por las mismas manos que torpemente me manoseaban; luego en un tipi en unos vastos llanos, donde aullaba el viento, contralto a las voces desquiciantes de los coyotes, con un joven que aún no se limpiaba la pintura de guerra de la cara, pero cuyas caricias tiernas desmentían la ferocidad con la cual acababa de arrancar diez pericráneos de las cabezas de los ojos borrados.

Quise decirte de esas otras vidas que me brotaban de la subconciencia y de las cuales estaba segura de haberlas vivido, pero siendo tú el aferrado cínico que eres en lo que atañe el ámbito espiritual, y en particular ante la reencarnación, sonreías tiernamente y entre largas inhalaciones de humo me decías que si cómo podía seguir creyendo en esas tonterías después de haberme explicado tantas veces lo de la base dialéctica y material de la existencia humana.

Y yo que no sé, que verdad que te creo y que todo lo que me has dado para leer lo he leído, y también lo creo pero de repente me vienen estas sensaciones de no sé dónde y son tan, cómo te diré, tan arrebatadoras, tan gruesas, y tan inmiscuidas en mi subconciencia que no puedo así nomás negarlas; vienen de la misma raíz de donde aquel sueño que siempre tenía de niña cuando me daba fiebre, y me veía con mis tías, todas en vestido de azul oscuro con lunares blancos, arrodilladas ante soldados romanos a caballo que nos daban latigazos en la espalda; de dónde crees que me venía ese sueño si yo nada sabía de Roma o de los romanos, todavía no leía, era la época pre-tele, todavía no tenía conocimiento del mundo y de su historia; de dónde tú crees que me venía; siempre me ha sido un misterio, y de esa misma raíz me vienen estas imágenes porque no pueden ser memorias, son más bien sensaciones, quizá sean memorias de la carne pero no del cerebro, cuando hago el amor...

Ay, cielo olvídate ya de ser tan histriónica, ahíncate en el análisis objetivo porque si no jamás saldrás de ese enmarañamiento de subjetividad que te ofusca la realidad material.

Ya, ya sé, pero no entiendes que yo no tengo control sobre este aspecto de mi ser; quizá surjan del hemisferio del lado derecho del cerebro, qué te parece...

Y tú con que ay, ya le das por otro lado; no ves que todo eso es la misma porquería, invenciones de cretinos para mantener al género humano en un estado perpetuo de ignorancia, para así poder llenar el globo de iglesias y de cosas y más cosas, de objetos, de mierda que no necesitamos pero sin las cuales no podríamos vivir porque a cada vuelta nos la aplastan en la cara, nos la meten en el cerebro y hasta en el culo para así mantener vivo un sistema anacrónico, deshumanizante que más valoriza un objeto que a un ser humano.

Yo sé, yo sé, te dije, pero mira cambiemos de tema porque yo sé que mi ignorancia te exaspera, pero créeme, mi amor, que quiero aprender de ti, que quiero que me llenes de ti, de tu cuerpo y de tus ideas y de todo lo que tú eres, pero ahora quiero hablar de otra cosa, quiero hablar del amor; ¿crees que es posible el amor?

Y tú, cautelosamente tratando de evitar la trampa, mira yo no sé si lo que tú y yo tenemos sea el amor; yo te quiero, te quiero, te quiero mucho, quiero estar siempre contigo, no me canso de hacer el amor contigo.

Y yo, volviendo a caer en *ese terreno peligroso de confundir el amor con la eternidad,* pero tú crees que

esto puede durar toda la vida, como el amor de mis
padres, el amor de mis abuelos; sabes que tengo unas
cartas que le escribió mi abuelo a mi abuela antes de
casarse; eran primos, sabes, primos carnales como
decimos nosotros allá, y vivían en el campo; las dos
familias vivían allí juntas, así que fue muy fácil que se
enamoraran; ella tenía trece años y él dieciocho cuando
se empezaron a escribir; es que tenían varios ranchos y a
él lo mandaban a trabajar a diferentes sitios; entonces él
le escribía y le mandaba las cartas con cualquier persona
que pasara por allí y, mira, le decía algo así:

*Créeme que cada día te quiero más y para el día 15
de julio sólo con la muerte te faltaré (*tú crees, sólo con
la muerte*). Deveras te quiero de todo corazón aun si
no fuera pecado más que a mi Dios (*a su mismo Dios,
imagínate*). Si tú me amaras tanto como yo a ti, ningún
cuchillo en este mundo podría quebrar nuestro amor.*

Qué bello, ¿verdad? quererse tanto y poder decirlo;
eso es lo difícil; tú por ejemplo nunca me dices cosas
así; yo creo que es porque hoy día expresamos nuestros
sentimientos físicamente y antes lo tenían que hacer con
puras palabras; tú te imaginas lo difícil que debe haber
sido ese amor, siendo ellos primos hermanos; en otra
carta le dice:

*Vida, dices que el padre nos casa como le dé la gana
por eso no hay cuidau (*sí, así lo escribió porque ya para
ese tiempo las escuelas eran en inglés y nuestra gente no
aprendió a escribir su lengua natal; escribían las cosas
como las decían) *que el padre pagándole no le importa
si todos los días se casan primos hermanos (*ya sabía que
esa parte te iba a gustar) *y no hay diferencia.*

Sí, así le decía; me las aprendí de memoria porque
me parecieron tan bellas y porque quería que fueran
parte de mí; pero parece que sí hubo diferencia y tuvieron
que solicitar permiso del arzobispo; lo que descubrimos
después de la muerte de mi abuela, que fue cuando
hallamos las cartas, fue que no se casaron en julio, sino
después y que su primera hija nació a los cinco meses,
¿tú crees? me imagino que lo que pasó fue que se les
negó el permiso y entonces decidieron forzar la cosa y

ella se embarazó; entonces qué iba a hacer la familia, porque era familia muy conocida por esos rumbos y muy respetada; bastante vergüenza les debe haber causado que se enamoraran estos dos primitos, pero cuando ella salió embarazada debe haber pagado buena cantidad la familia para que se hiciera todo respetablemente; así que mi promiscuidad, vida, me viene en la sangre. Y seguí insistiendo, y tú, me quieres tanto como mi abuelo a mi abuela; sacrificarías tu honra y tu vida por mí; no me digas, ya lo sé, eso sólo por la lucha de clases; y mira, Sergio, eso de hacerme un niñito, ni lo pienses porque todavía para mi generación corre el peligro del rabito de puerco—por el pecado de mis abuelos ¿sabes?

Mis padres, pues, no eran primos, pero fíjate que sí
tenían el mismo apellido. Así que vengo siendo Martínez
por lado de mi abuelo paterno, mi abuela paterna y mi
abuelo materno. Pero aunque no fueran primos, desde
niños se conocían y se querían y cuando tenían 28 años se
huyeron y se casaron sin que nadie lo supiera. Al papá de
mi padre casi le dio un infarto puesto que consideraba a
mi mamá demasiado inferior para su hijo. Para mi mamá,
eso de casarse clandestinamente fue un poco increíble
ya que siempre sufrió de esa enfermedad insípida que
llaman "el qué dirán."

La verdad es que es una mujer admirable a pesar
de que en la superficie parezca de lo más ordinario. Me
acuerdo de cuando ella, aun joven, se pasaba todo el
día cantando y entrándole al trabajo igual que papi en
la huerta, en los corrales, techando nuestra casita. Pero
antes de eso fue maestra y después lo volvió a ser, hecho
que en sí resulta fuera de lo común dadas las condiciones
sociales de su época. Ella era de una familia pobre; su
papá murió cuando tenía siete años y su mamá no tuvo
más recurso que salir a limpiarles las casas a los gabachos
y a lavarles y plancharles la ropa. Cuenta mi mamá que
vivían en un jacalito a la orilla del pueblito que tenía un
piso de tablas. Entre las rendijas se veían serpientes que
vivían debajo del jacalito y cada mañana su mamá les
echaba agua hirviente.

Las paredes las cubrían con periódicos y a medida
que iba aprendiendo a leer, ella les leía de los periódicos
a sus hermanitos. Cuando fue a la escuela, no sabía ni
siquiera una palabra de inglés pero como no les permitían
usar el español muy pronto aprendían los niños el inglés,
a lo trochi mochi, como dice papi. Cuando estaba en el
tercer año, tenía una maestra que tocaba el piano y que
a mami la trataba con mucho cariño. Fue entonces, tú
crees Sergio, a los ocho años, que decidió mi mamá que

cuando fuera grande iba a ser maestra y a tocar el piano. Sí, esa misma niña que desde su cama veía culebras debajo de la casa. Pues cuando terminó la secundaria a los diecisiete años, consiguió un puesto de maestra en un pueblito que quedaba a doscientas millas de su pueblo natal. Aceptó porque lo vio como una oportunidad de ayudarle a su mamá para que ya no tuviera que lavar pisos de rodillas. Al despedirse de mi padre no le permitió besarla porque creía que eso era algo que sólo se debía hacer entre casados. Su inocencia era tal que cuando le empezó la regla, se atemorizó tanto que corrió y se metió en la acequia y allí estuvo todo el día hasta que tuvo que entrar mi abuelita y sacarla a la fuerza. Y, allí iba, imagínate, tan inocente y solita, a lo que debe haberle parecido la orilla del mundo, a hacerse la vida.

Durante los próximos diez años fue maestra en escuelas rurales enseñándoles a leer y a escribir a jóvenes que en los primeros años de su carrera tenían casi su misma edad. Se me hace que la veo ahora mismo, menudita y medio tímida, pero de una fuerza interior increíble, dándoles azotes a los muchachones que se portaban mal en el aula. Y se compró un piano usado pero sólo aprendió a tocar "Las cuatro milpas." Aun hoy día se sienta ante su piano antiguo a tocar la única canción de su repertorio; se le llenan de luz los ojos y veo que pasa ante ella toda su vida como película en cámara lenta. Creo que en ese momento siente que más allá de sus cinco hijas, esa canción es la única cosa en el mundo que verdaderamente le pertenece. Bueno, eso y su profunda fe en la Virgen María.

Después de casarse se fueron a vivir en el ranchito de los tíos que criaron a papi. Aun hoy hablan de esa época de su vida como su residencia en el paraíso terrestre. Durante la guerra perdieron su rancho y se fueron a vivir al pueblo y después a México por dos años cuando el gobierno de Estados Unidos reclutó a rancheros mexicanos del Sudoeste para ir a trabajar en la AFTOSA. Creo que ha sido la única vez que se haya reconocido oficialmente el valor del español de los chicanos. Claro, todos los gerentes y los jefes de los equipos estadounidenses eran bolillos y los peones los "Mexican-Americans," pero sin éstos jamás podrían haber entrado a los pueblitos mexicanos a inocular ganado. Papi, por ejemplo, llegaba a algún pueblito como Tala. Se iba directamente con el cura y le explicaba su misión. El domingo iba a misa y el cura lo presentaba a los parroquianos urgiéndoles que cooperaran con él. El lunes empezaban a vacunar las vacas y las cabras de los aldeanos y de allí seguían a los ranchos.

Cuando regresamos de México, se enfermó papi y no pudo trabajar por algún tiempo. Mami volvió a ser maestra y ésa fue su carrera que desempeñó hasta jubilarse hace unos años. En cierto sentido mi mamá permanece un enigma para mí. Siempre la vi tan dependiente emocionalmente de mi padre, y a la vez sé que tuvo tremenda voluntad y fuerza interior. Toda la vida la agobiaron temores y dudas; sin embargo aprendió a funcionar en un ambiente ajeno y hostil (digo, el ambiente de los americanos) y ésa fue la herencia que nos dio. Y nosotras, yo y mis hermanas, siempre estuvimos loquitas con papi. Cada una quería ser el hijo que nunca tuvo, manifestando una competencia feroz por sus atenciones. A mami la ignorábamos. Era natural que ella hiciera todo el trabajo de casa además de su trabajo fuera de casa, trabajo que seguía haciendo para que tuviéramos vestidos y zapatos nuevos para la Navidad y para poder mandarnos a la universidad. Ahora que reflejo sobre la historia de mi familia, veo a mi madre como una roca fuerte y estable que brota de la tierra y se impone imperiosamente sobre el paisaje de mi vida.

Ay, perdóname amor que te aburra con todo esto. Es que me dio un ataque de nostalgia. Además quiero ser para ti un libro abierto. No sé por qué, pero siento una profunda necesidad de contártelo todo.

DAMAS Y CABALLEROS, su atención por favor. Les ha tocado a ustedes la maravillosa fortuna de viajar en este tren precisamente en este momento ya que aquí en esta maleta llevo una verdadera ganga. Estimados señores y señoras, quizá sea la ganga de su vida. Estas estampas de Nuestro Señor crucificado son de la más fina calidad que jamás se haya presentado en el mercado público. Acabo de conseguirlas en los Estados Unidos, donde adornan las iglesias más hermosas y modernas del país. Fíjense nomás, caros amigos, en los bellos detalles, las facciones perfectas de Nuestro Señor. Mírenle los ojos. ¿No es verdad que reflejan el más puro y perfecto amor? A ver cuántas se llevan. Sólo a quince pesos. No pierdan esta única oportunidad. Sólo me quedan veinte, las últimas veinte del mundo. En los Esteits se han agotado y a México sólo han llegado las que su humilde servidor les ofrece. A ver señor, ¿se lleva una? señorita, ¿usted cuántas? Compren una bella estampa de nuestro redentor para que adorne y bendiga su humilde hogar.

¿Cuándo fue que nos vimos? ¿Apenas cuatro días? No lo creo. Sabes que cuando paso un día sin verte, te extraño tanto que me quiero morir. ¿Verdad que apenas hace cuatro días? A mí se me hizo más. Pero sabes que también me gusta cuando no nos vemos por algún tiempo porque siempre son mucho más intensos mis orgasmos. No sé, duran más. Hoy por ejemplo fue increíble, como una torrente de ola tras ola de espasmos eléctricos. Creí que nunca iba a terminar. ¿Te imaginas lo que sería quedarse uno atascado en un orgasmo perpetuo? Sería algo así como las personas que no pueden dejar de estornudar, placer y agonía. En términos puramente biológicos, el estornudar es semejante al orgasmo, ¿no te parece? A mí, por ejemplo, me encanta estornudar. Siento gran satisfacción y placer al hacerlo.

Sabes que el primero, digo el primer orgasmo, siempre es fantástico, ¿no? Claro, porque es el descargo de una tremenda acumulación de energía, pero de ninguna manera se le acerca ni en intensidad ni en satisfacción al segundo o al tercero. No sé cómo explicarlo, pero éstos parecen originar en un sitio mucho más profundo que el primero, especialmente si vienen bien seguiditos. A veces siento que brotan del mero centro de mi ser físico y espiritual. No te rías. No sé cómo más explicarlo. La verdad es que es imposible describir la sensación pero, *sans doute*, vale la pena, aunque a veces cueste tanto trabajo lograrla. Dime la verdad, ¿no te dan celitos que yo pueda tener un montón de orgasmos sin esperar, digo, sin recuperarme del primero? La otra noche estábamos hablando Toña, Lupe, Isaura y yo, y decidimos que el patriarcado se debe al orgasmo múltiple del género femenino. Estoy hablando en serio.

Mira, si la hembra es capaz de tener múltiples orgasmos, ¿qué le va a impedir que se largue con otro mientras el primero se recupera? Claro, después habría un lío con que quién es el padre—pero eso ya es otra cosa. Así que tú lo ves más bien como asunto de la herencia de la propiedad privada. Bueno, eso ya lo sé, pero de ninguna manera disminuye la posibilidad de que exista alguna relación entre la posición social (not to mention la posición supina en el acto conyugal) de la mujer y su propensidad al orgasmo múltiple.

Mira, creo que cuando el hombre, Adán o quién fuese, se dio cuenta de esta dádiva femenina, se percató de lo difícil que sería controlar a su Evita querida. (A lo mejor tengas razón, y sí fue Segismundito, pero me imagino que ya andaba rodando por allí esta información en los tiempos de Adán). Pucha, hasta con la serpiente era capaz de escabullirse la malagradecida. Así que ¿qué hacer? Según mi interpretación puramente personal, se ofrecían dos soluciones. Una: negarle a la mujer esos múltiples orgasmos, haciéndola creer que el único orgasmo genuino era el orgasmo inducido por el órgano masculino inyectado en el receptáculo femenino.

Ahora bien, si no quedaba satisfecha, y puesto que él tenía que recuperarse, ¿cómo permitir métodos heterodoxos (deditos, lengüitas, etc.)? Ni modo, porque esto le daría a ella la idea que su placer no dependía de you know what...el instrumento sagrado. Seguía que cualquier mujer insatisfecha con un sólo orgasmo, claro, vía el coito, *non erat mulierem integram*. Ahora bien, como siempre existía la posibilidad de que hubiera por allí rebeldes, digamos, chicas inclinadas a salir en pos de más, en pos de variedad, había que herrarla de alguna manera para que permaneciera estigmatizada —claro, por su gula orgásmica— ante el mundo.

Solución número dos: acuñar sustantivo denigrante y acusador. (¿De qué? Pues de mujer adicta al placer del orgasmo múltiple). ¡Right on, cachetón! LA PUTA. Con esta palabrita de cuatro letras, junto con el mito del exclusivo orgasmo, tipo pene-(preferiblemente el del esposo)-en-la-vagina, se controló el comportamiento lascivo de Evita, y Adancito quedó libre para hacerla de Don Juan. Relacionado a esto podríamos comentar el fenómeno de que no existe la forma femenina de cornudo. O sea, que la mujer que tiene más de un hombre le pone cuernos a su compañero, hecho imperdonable y de infinita vergüenza para la víctima encornada. Sin embargo, hombre que tiene mujeres extracurriculares no le pone ni cuernos ni nada a su esposa o compañera; *au contraire*, a él se le adula de ser todo un hombre; y de la esposa, en algún momento (específicamente en el velorio del esposo) se dirá que fue una santa.

Además, se podría comentar que relacionado a *este* curioso fenómeno lingüístico/cultural, existe otro no menos curioso; a saber, que no existe el equivalente masculino de ninfomaníaca. Bueno eso de sátiro ya lo había anticipado. A ver, ¿tú dime si jamás has oído en conversación común y corriente a alguien llamar sátiro al hombre más lascivo en dado universo de discurso? Ahora dime ¿a cuántas niñas ninfomaníacas conoces? Por lo menos 139. ¡Ay chavo, con qué fineza complementas mis discursos! Y para resumir: mujer dada a la promiscuidad = Puta, ninfomaníaca y colocadora de cuernos. Todos signos negativos y acusadores. No obstante, a varón del mismo corte se le glorifica y se le tiene de ídolo cultural.

Es verdad, me he desviado un poco del tema original. Sin embargo, todo tiene que ver con todo. Ahora, lo único que me queda decir referente a ello es que lo que nos hace falta a las mujeres, es explorar y desarrollar el orgasmo múltiple, haciendo de él la base de una nueva ideología política. Ya me lo imaginaba. A ti te encanta la idea porque no hay nada que más te guste que facilitarme cuanto orgasmo apetezca, a como dé lugar, con o sin pene. ¿Y estás seguro que nada de complejitos por tu parte? Ay, Sergio sois una verdadera joya.

Alaaaaaaaaaaaaaarma. Ay, perdón señorita, no se alarme. Es que vendo la revista *Alarma*. Se compra una, ¿verdad? Ándele, así no se aburre en el viaje. Mire aquí lo que dice: CRIATURA DE DOS CABEZAS NACE EN JOJUTLA. Újule mano, eso es el colmo. Y aquí, mire: LA COCAINA LE HA PODRIDO LA NARIZ A RICHARD BURTON. A poco. Pos le tendrán que poner una nariz postiza. Y mire, mire, esto le debe interesar siendo usted pocha: AUMENTAN LAS DROGAS EN D.F. DEBIDO A LOS JIPES NORTEAMERICANOS. Y mire esta foto, ¡híjole qué cuerote! Cállate malcriado y pásame una. Gracias señorita, no le va a pesar.

...Bueno esta lectura alumbradora requiere un buen cigarrillo mexicano y el silencio de mi cabina. A ver si consigo dormir un rato después de leer esta porquería...

...Ay Dios, ¿quién llama a esta hora? Será Lencho. Qué muchacho tan terco. Sólo porque intercambiamos unas palabras —bueno, la verdad es que tuvimos una larga e interesante conversación a la hora de la cena y no es tan grueso como me lo imaginaba— ya se le hace que somos novios...

¿Quién es?

Soy yo, Lencho. Abre, por favor. Es que necesito que me hagas un favorcito.

...Favorcito, fuchi, los rodeos que les damos a las cosas...

Ya es tarde Lencho y quiero dormir.

Por favor, pochita. Es importante.

...Bueno, sí tuvo la cortesía de arreglarme el excusado después de la parada en Aguascalientes y a pesar de que tenía un montón de otras cosas que hacer. Verdad que le debo uno, pero si me ataca el bruto, primero le pico los ojos, y luego le doy un rodillazo donde mero mero...

Por Dios, ¿qué quieres a estas horas?

Mira, pochita, ¿podría dejar esta cajita en tu alcoba hasta la mañana? La recojo al llegar al D.F.

Ni modo. Yo no te voy a esconder quién sabe qué porquería en mi alcoba. ¿Por qué no la escondes en la tuya?

No puedo. Es que el jefe nos esculca todo. Anda, no te hagas de rogar. No es nada más que un regalito de la frontera que le llevo a mi chava. Si lo halla el jefón me lo quita y se lo lleva a su vieja.

Ándale, déjalo y lárgate de aquí, que si no duermo un par de horas esta noche, llego hecha una porquería mañana.

Y eso, ni modo, ¿verdad, pochita? Hay que llegar bien guapita para enamorar a todos los chavos del

D.F., ¿verdad? Te advierto que todos son una bola de maricones, así que no te hagas ilusiones. Para hombres, cielito, no hay como los de Chihuahua. Pero eso lo tendrás que descubir para ti misma.

Si no se te haga que no me he dado cuenta que ustedes los de *shi*huahua se las hacen de muy Pancho Villa. Pues mira, si acaso no lo sabes mano, ya Pancho Villa está fuera de moda. El estilo ahora ya no es ranchero. Ya nos tenemos otro héroe latino. A saber, se llama Che. Pero tú qué vas a saber armadillo del desierto.

¡Ay, qué chispa tienes pochita! Se me para −el corazón− al oírte hablar así. Qué lástima que no seas como las beibis güeras. Si lo fueras, tú y yo haríamos *gud taim tugedor tunait.*

Lencho, a ver si te mides esto (gesto obsceno), a lo mejor te venga bien (Cierra la puerta de golpe).

...Isque regalito para su chava. Ni que fuera retrasada mental. ¿Qué será? Claro, son instrumentos y libretitas pornográficas. A lo mejor es una pistola y este cretino esté pensando matar y desmembrarme y después echarme por la ventana −primero un piecito, luego la oreja izquierda, un mechón de cabellos, el brazo derecho. DAMN IT! WILL YOU STOP!

Lo obvio m'ija es que son drogas y tú la muy mensa se las vas a acarrear. No dudaría que al llegar al D.F. te pidiera que le entregaras la cajita a su novia porque no le dieron los días de descanso prometidos y el tren sale a Juárez en diez minutos. ¿Sabes lo que se hará de ti si te descubre la policía acarreando drogas? Sí, m'ija, derechito a Lecumberri a podrirte con los demás jipes endrogados. Újule, las llamaditas a tus padres, que si no nos mandan diez mil dólares la ponemos en libertad, luego que cinco mil más, después, que no se puede, que tendrán que venir ustedes para hacer los trámites, y los meses se harán años y cada día te saldrá otra cana, y los guardias abusarán de ti según les dicte su desmesurada lujuria, y un invierno húmedo, de esos que sólo en la región más transparente se dan, te hallarán tiesecita con los pulmones podridos (y no como resultado de los cochinos cigarrillos, pues ésos ya hará mucho tiempo que los habrás dejado por falta de recursos económicos).

Estimados señores pochos del otro lado:

Sentimos tener que avisarles por medio de ésta que su hija, la preciosa pochita que diez años pasó en Lecumberri, ha muerto de tuberculosis...

Ay, pero ¿quién llama otra vez y a esta hora?
¿Quién es?
Señorita, abra por favor, vengo con un recado de Lencho. Dice que me dé la cajita.
¿Estás loco o se te han zafado las tuercas con las vibraciones del tren?
Fíjese que no, señorita. Dice Lencho que es muy importante que me la dé.
Pues toma, y dile que ya no me vuelva a molestar con su pinche caja. ¡NECESITO DORMIR!
...Pero estos cigarrillos mexicanos huelen a estiércol, uuuy, y saben peor que el estiércol. Bueno, ya me acostumbraré. ¿Qué se traerán esos pobres desgraciados, que aquí está la cajita, que ya no está la cajita. A ver cuando me caen con conejitos blancos. La verdad es que tengo tanto sueño que no me importa un pito...

...El tren se detiene a la orilla de un promontorio que se proyecta hacia el centro de las aguas de un enorme lago. Ella se asoma por la ventanilla y en la distancia ve un pueblo que parece estar suspendido sobre el mero corazón del lago. Se viste de prisa, arrebata sus maletas y abandona su cabina. En el pasillo se topa con Lencho quien estira los brazos para no dejarla pasar. Ella se da una rápida vuelta para huir en sentido opuesto pero ya su cintura se encuentra envuelta en los brazos agresivos de Lencho quien, acercando los labios a su oído, le suplica que se quede en el tren mientras desembarcan los demás pasajeros. Su aliento es una llama encendida que la envuelve en un trance hipnótico. Sus manos ya se mueven hábilmente debajo del suéter rojo de ella y su sexo erecto le acosa las nalgas como bastón de ciego buscando la puerta de un edificio desconocido. Ella siente que le baja una espesa oleada de jugo lubricante e instintivamente empieza a ondular en un lento y deliberado ritmo las caderas amplias contra el enorme órgano rígido que demanda apertura. De pronto se acuerda que el tren se ha detenido y piensa que seguramente estarán en el D.F. Se desliza como gelatina blanda de los brazos de Lencho y con los pechos erectos apuntando el camino corre hacia la puerta del vagón.

La luz de la mañana le hiere los ojos desvelados y apenas evita resbalarse en el escalón. Cuando por fin recupera su visión normal empieza a divisar el movimiento de un hermoso e intricado calidoscopio humano que se despliega en una danza improvisada por las calles amplias y limpias. Cientos de jóvenes descalzos y en taparrabos que apenas les cubren las partes privadas se deslizan por el andén como patinadores olímpicos, ofreciendo alquilar canoas y andas a los recién llegados. Muchachas en huipiles blancos y trenzas negras atadas con listones de todos los matices del arco iris pregonan mangos, piñas, camotes, elotes cocidos y cuánto más se le ofrezca al viajero cansado. Ella camina despacio, abriéndose brecha por la multitud de gente que remolina al ritmo de un tambor interior en turno suyo. Los olores de la calle, de la mercancía y de los cuerpos apresurados le asaltan la nariz y siente ganas de vomitar.

De pronto se clavan dos enanos ante ella, los dos en taparrabos blancos y cinturones verdes y rosados. Le informan que su señora los ha despachado a recogerla y le indican que se suba en la canoa cubierta por un pabellón adornado con plumas verdes y bordados de plata. Estupefacta ante el carnaval que pulula frente a sus ojos, los cuales se percatan de haber vivido en la deprivación sensual más abyecta hasta el momento de desbordar el tren, obedece sin decir palabra. No sabe a dónde la llevan los enanitos joviales, pero a la vez se siente impulsada por una fuerza oculta a acompañarlos.

Caminan varias horas por canoa a lo largo de una amplia calzada que une el promontorio con la ciudad distante cuyas torres y edificios de albañilería impresionante relumbran bajo el sol tropical. Al llegar a tierra firme, la canoa pasa a uno de los muchos canales que atraviesan la ciudad como banquetas líquidas, y a cuyas orillas se levantan viviendas de tezontli rojo y de adobes encalados, de uno y de dos pisos, cada una con su jardín frondoso en la azotea. Con cada remada se acercan a los blancos teocallis que se erigen como espejismo contra un enorme fondo de azul transparente. Atónita, ella mira de un lado a otro pensando que lo que ve es sueño porque ve cosas que jamás había imaginado o visto, ni siquiera soñado.

Que no es sueño se lo prueba su delicado sentido del olfato al recibir el aroma de gruesas capas de sangre putrefacta que adornan las escaleras de los templos sagrados. Como si esto no fuera bastante desconcierto para la recién llegada, entra a su campo de vista un ábaco enorme cuyos centenares de cuentas consisten en calaveras grotescas apiladas sobre estacas de bambú cual gárgolas siniestras en guardia muda y caprichosa. Se repite por segunda vez esa mañana el impulso de vaciar todo el contenido del estómago por la boca. Tan pronto como aparece esta reacción física, desaparece y ella concentra la atención en la escena que se despliega lenta y maravillosamente al pasar la canoa por un arco labrado en el muro de lo que después se enterará es uno de los castillos del gran señor de Tenochtitlán. La canoa desemboca en un enorme jardín que reposa tranquilo entre los cuatro muros del magnífico castillo. Al desembarcar, la espera una señora cuyo aspecto noble se revela en su vestir y en su presencia. ¡Qué bella eres! Entona con entusiasmo. Muy consciente he estado yo de que mi comportamiento produciría una bella y fuerte raza. El verte me complace y me compensa los insultos y los latigazos que sobre mi persona colmará la historia.[1]

1   Marina was at this time in the morning of life. She is said to have possessed uncommon personal attractions* and her open, expressive features indicated her generous temper. She always remained faithful to the countrymen of her adoption; and her knowledge and customs of the Mexicans, and often of their designs, enabled her to extricate Spaniards, more than once, from the most embarrassing and perilous situations. She had her errors, as we have seen. But they should be rather charged to the defects of early education, and to the evil influence of him to whom in the darkness of her spirit she looked with simple confidence for the light to guide her. All agree that she was full of excellent qualities, and the important services which she rendered the Spaniards have made her memory deservedly dear to them; while the name of Malinche–*the name by which she is still known in Mexico was pronounced with kindness by the conquered races, with whose misfortunes she showed an invariable sympathy:*

        *Admire tan lúcida cabalgada
        Y espectáculo Doña Marina
        India Noble al caudillo presentada,
        De fortuna y belleza peregrina

        Con despejado espíritu y viveza
        Gira la vista en el concurso mudo;
        Rico manto de extrema sutileza
        Con chapas de oro autorizarla pudo,

        Prendido con bizarra gentileza

Tomándola del brazo, empiezan las dos a caminar por el jardín. La señora sigue pronunciando un largo discurso en una voz, ahora serena, que contrasta agudamente con el contenido de su mensaje.

Mari, has tenido buena fortuna en llegar antes de la destrucción eminente de esta hermosa ciudad. De todo lo que has visto hoy, los templos, los mercados, los palacios, este jardín, sólo quedarán escombros testimoniales. Estos extranjeros que nos han mandado nuestros dioses son una plaga destructiva. Aunque son pocos en comparación a la extensión de nuestro pueblo, su triunfo es inexorable. Aun si nuestro gran señor estuviera en condiciones de actuar decisivamente y se detuviera esta oleada golosa de hombres que escupen fuego, vendrían otros, y otros y, en fin, tropas de ellos para arrancar la última flor de nuestra raza, mandando a cada uno de nosotros a reposar en las tinieblas de Mictlan. El fin de nuestro mundo tal como lo conocemos es inevitable; sin embargo es posible e imprescindible poner a salvo lo que podamos. La nuestra es una raza hermosa, fuerte y fecunda. No obstante, hay algunos entre nosotros que se empeñan en destruirla con luchas intestinas; estamos atrapados y clavados en el círculo del tiempo debido a la constante brega, a causa del hambre por el maldito poder y el deseo de mantener este nivel de opulencia. Si los come-zoquete emplumados de las provincias no produjeran con el puro sudor de sus espaldas, comida y mercancía, si no extrajeran los recursos de nuestra madre, no sería posible que los distinguidos águilas y jaguares vivieran así; y para asegurar este orden hay que conquistar y dividir, hay que imponer la guerra perpetua.

Y ahora estos falsos teules se aprovecharán de nuestra desunidad para derrotarnos. Nuestros jefes, Mari, cuánto dolor me da tener que decirlo, son débiles,

---

Sobre los pechos en ayroso nudo;
Reyna parece de la Indiana Zona,
Varonil y hermosísima Amazona.

o de cuerpo o de mente. Algunos quieren luchar para guardar el momento; ésos son los débiles de mente porque no entienden que eso provocará la ira y la gula de estos bárbaros. El príncipe Cuauhtémoc, por ejemplo, resistirá hasta que le quemen los pies y los futuros creadores de mitos le brindarán homenaje y le edificarán monumentos, pero lo que no admitirán los historiadores es que aun si triunfara El Águila que Cae, su triunfo sería del momento porque, por fin, el Rey de ultramar mandaría a su último vasallo a destruir a nuestra raza.

Me parece que el reino de ese cacique don Fernando está en condiciones de fracaso. Sus gentes se encuentran en un estado de profunda congoja. Los agobia el saber que viven en un callejón sin salida. Están atrapados en modelos caducos y sus antiguos mitos van perdiendo su significado cósmico. Por todos lados buscan salida de ese pozo que los circunda y éste, nuestro mundo, será su salvación. El hecho de que vienen armados de profundas dudas, los forzará a destruir nuestro mundo...con espada, con cruz, con falo. Y Moctezuma, pobrecito mi gran señor del bastón chueco, lo tienen de los cuates los sacerdotes con su magia y su superstición; tiene el alma más noble que jamás pisara esta tierra, pero es débil, y el temor a los dioses lo hará colaborar con ellos, Mari, pero escúchame bien. Quiero que comprendas mis acciones para que algún día cuando te hiera la violencia de las palabras, "Hijo de la chingada," entiendas los motivos que me impulsan. Mira las mujeres en esta sociedad, igual que lo serán en la tuya, son meros objetos, son muebles, son la propiedad de sus padres y después de sus esposos. El único honor que se les otorga en esta cultura, es ser sacrificadas, siempre que sean vírgenes. ¡Gran honor!

Mira, los sacerdotes, los príncipes, los mercaderes, los artesanos, los guerreros, todos son varones. Las mujeres somos primero los espejos que reflejan la imagen del varón para que se percate de quién es; después somos sus juguetes en el petate y, en fin, receptáculos e incubadoras de sus granos de maíz. Se nos relega al mundo de la sombra y del silencio; pero ese silencio engendra la palabra que se revuelca en nuestra misma hiel y se vuelve rencor, injuria y también canto; y a esta palabra se le agrega otra y otra y terminan en fin siendo una larga y fuerte cadena que nos envuelve y nos estrangula. Podemos rendirnos ante ella, expirar asfixiadas de palabras que nunca encontraron voz, o podemos conjurar, con todos los agüeros del cielo y del infierno, esa voz y volcarla sobre el mundo de los grandes señores. Ante ella, ellos recularán en temor y demostrarán sus verdaderas tendencias –la soledad, la reticencia oculta tras máscaras y órganos sexuales que disparan cual arcos y flechas, arcabuces y escopetas. ¿Te imaginas, Mari, si se uniera cada una de las cadenas de palabras de cada una de las mujeres del mundo, el poder que se generaría? Y ese poder lo podríamos encauzar hacia la creación de una sociedad donde todos anduvieran desnudos, sin vergüenza, sin mentiras o flaquezas a esconder: una sociedad donde se dividiera la labor y los frutos de esa labor y de nuestra madre tierra; una sociedad donde todos, hombre y mujer, se encargaran de nutrir y de educar a nuestras hijas y a nuestros hijos para que aprendieran a obrar con gracia, con honradez, con creatividad y con compasión humana. Las mujeres somos fuertes, Mari; nuestra fuerza nos viene del silencio impuesto por manos sociales y legales que nos tapan la boca.

Mira, yo me encuentro en la encrucijada de un camino traicionero. Me sigue una historia de infamia y de degradación. No una, sino dos veces he sido vendida como mercancía corriente, una por mi madre y otra, como lonja de carne, por mi señor quien, en cambio, esperaba recibir el buen favor de Cortés. ¡Ah, Cortés! Llegamos por fin a hablar de mi amante de las piernas chuecas, de esa bestia de los dioses blancos, astuto blandidor de espada, maestro del juego y de la manipulación, anhelador persistente de la gloria y de la fama.

Desde el principio reconocí en sus ojos esa chispa que impulsa a los seres humanos a cometer los actos más desesperados en el camino de la ascendencia. Por todos lados veía a nuestros caciques vacilar ante él, que no era dios, que sí era dios, que tal vez fuera dios. Yo decidí poner fin a sus cavilaciones. Me acosté con él y he descubierto que hace el amor como cualquier hombre mortal, a la brava y acomplejado por las limitaciones de su instrumento. Y también he descubierto su proclividad al poder. He resuelto aliarme con él para absorber ese poder que ciertamente será suyo y así alterar el destino de mi pueblo que se encuentra encaminado hacia la aniquilación. Me sirvo de la fuerza de mi voz y se la ofrezco a Cortés, convirtiéndome en su lengua y en su alcahueta. Sí, el necesario eslabón entre su mundo y el nuestro. Mi objeto es ayudarle a lograr sus imperiosos designios mediante la palabra y el compromiso. Veo ésta como la única vía a la salvación de nuestra raza, porque eso es lo que más me obsesiona en este momento tan crítico. Por mi culpa, han muerto muchos, en Cholula, miles de guerreros bravos, y morirán muchos más antes de que esto haya terminado.

Pero, en fin, si mi colaboración con este diablo hechicero es necesaria para asegurar que no muramos todos, yo estoy dispuesta a venderme a mí misma. ¿Qué más da repetir lo ya conocido? Pero en este caso mi venta es el resultado del ejercicio de mi voluntad, la cual no me permite acceder pasivamente al atropello total de mi raza. Mi acto de traición, que así lo marcará la historia, promete insertar el germen de nuestra flor en el nuevo orden que inmutablemente se diseminará con los cuatro vientos. Sin mi acto de colaboración, desaparecería nuestra raza y se daría en este imperio la raza pura de los teules falsos, débil y anímica ante la grandeza, la majestad y el capricho de nuestro ambiente. Sin embargo, debido a mis acciones, se dará una nueva raza mestiza en cuyas venas fluirá la fuerza de mi sangre, de mi voluntad y de mi palabra femenina. Tú, Mari, eres el futuro fruto de mi vientre, la flor de mi traición.

Desde dentro, desde fuera, yo, tú, ella, Mari. ¿Cómo narrar un sueño? ¿Es la soñadora la narradora? ¿Es la camarógrafa? ¿Es también la soñada? ¿La actriz? La soñadora está fuera viendo el sueño. Se ve a sí misma, así que también está dentro. Está fuera y está dentro. Desde fuera percibe la acción visualmente como observadora omnisciente. Desde dentro se siente observada desde fuera por sí misma. Se siente lejos, distanciada de lo soñado; se siente cerca, emocionalmente ligada a la acción. ¿Qué diferencia hay entre el sueño y la narración?

Señorita, abra por favor. Le habla el Capitán Acevedo. Abra la puerta. Señorita, la puerta, por favor. No tenemos toda la noche.

...¡Ay Dios! ¿Quién me despierta a las dos de la mañana? A poco ya vienen con la maldita caja..... Vete a la fregada, Lencho, y déjame dormir.

Perdone señorita que hayamos entrado así a la fuerza, pero es que tenemos que revisar todas las alcobas. Me haría el favor de salir al pasillo.

¿Pero, cómo? ¿Qué derecho tienen ustedes.....?

Señorita mejor sería callar esa boquita pintada y hacer lo que le mando. Así no andamos después con bracitos rotos, ¿eh?

...Is this guy for real? Is this damn trip for real? Maybe I'm really a character in an Agatha Christie script, riding the Orient Express and don't even know it. Jesus, that fly speck is going through my stuff as if he owned it...

Gracias señorita y perdone la molestia. Ya puede volverse a dormir. Buenas noches.

...Ay, qué gracioso, isque me vuelva a dormir. ¿Dónde estarán esos malditos cigarrillos? Y todo esto, ¿a qué se debe? Es verdad que han tenido problemas con los campesinos y ha tenido que intervenir el ejército, pero eso es en las montañas. Además estos buscaban algo –algo específico. ¡La maldita caja de Lencho! Tiene que haber sido eso. A ver qué me cuenta por la mañana. Ahora no queda más remedio que fumarme estas porquerías...

Se quedó así durante un largo tiempo, la cara pegada al acero frío, las manos apretando fuertemente las dos varitas de hierro que corrían a cada lado del techo. Sentía un fuerte deseo de voltearse boca arriba para contemplar las miles de estrellas bordadas en la cúpula negra que cubría el desierto pero el temor que sentía de ser descubierto lo forzó a permanecer inmóvil, paralizado, los músculos contraídos, fuertes y duros como el mismo acero.

...Desgraciados, puercos, cómo se están tardando. Ya los veo buscando hasta en el excusado. Gracias a Dios que la sacamos de la alcoba de la pochita. No sé cómo se me ocurrió ponerla en tanto peligro. Qué chistosa chava. Se las hace de muy matona pero en realidad se esconde detrás de una gruesa máscara porque no sabe quién es. Pero quién lo fuera a saber viviendo atrapado entre dos mundos, en un limbo, como lo hacen los pochos. Cuánto hace que los olvidó México y allí siguen, siempre marginados. Por mucho que se esfuercen en ser como los gabas, siempre quedan fuera, prendidos al tejido del alambre del cerco de la ilusión mirando hacia dentro con ojos y boca de niño hambriento ante la vidriera de una dulcería. A veces creo que la pasan mejor los pelados de allá. Por lo menos ellos saben quiénes son; hormigas trabajadoras, complaciéndose con cualquier migaja de pan, porque al fin y al cabo es el pan en la barriguita de sus niños lo que cuenta. Ni siquiera se acercan a la muralla de ilusión. Si no aprenden el inglés, qué más da, por todos lados se habla español. Si no se educan sus hijos, qué más da; a poco la educación les va a hacer un hoyito en el cerco de ilusión. Los pocos hoyos que se permiten ya están señalados para los pochos más astutos, los que han olvidado su lengua nativa, los que en un momento hacen maromas o lo que se les pida para probar que merecen existir dentro del círculo mágico.

Creo que por eso es que vino la pochita a Mexicles. El puro temor de ser sifonada por una pequeña hendidura al círculo vacío la impulsa a regresar a sus raíces en busca de una pequeña semilla de identidad. Pobrecita pochita, qué desengaño va a sufrir al descubrir otra muralla de ilusión. Cuántas ganas me dieron de decirle de una vez que a los mexicanos les importa un comino la otra cara de México. Están allá porque son una bola de pinches traicioneros, y eso es todo. Si les va mal, pues allá ellos; a quién se le ocurre irse a sufrir allá, a recibir las bofetadas y el escupo de los gringos. Mejor sufrir en jacal propio que en palacio ajeno. Pero ni modo, se la merecen esos pollos, borregas, acarreados, mojas, alambres, wetbacks, hormigas, aventureros, despatriados. Y los que vendió Santa Anna –de esos no saben nada los mexicanos. Creen que todos se volvieron gringos al firmarse el Tratado de Guadalupe Hidalgo. La verdad es que el único mexicano que existe del otro lado es maldito malinchista.

Pero no me atreví a decirle palabra de todo eso a la pochita para no destruirle la inocente ilusión que la impulsa a este país de mierda que cada día entierra a sus hijos con barrigas hinchadas de hambre, o peor aún, los empuja a puras patadas hacia el elusivo dorado. Mejor me mordí la lengua e hice el papelón de machón pendejo, igual que lo hacemos ante las güeras, queriendo así vengarnos de no sé qué, quizás del amo extranjero que nos chupa la sangre y nos deja tirados y encuerados para que después nos capen como a pinches animales nuestros mismitos jefes –soy tu padre, cabrón y por eso te dejo sin más testículos que los que tú mismo te puedas inventar, y entre más grandes mejor, porque ésos son los que más les gustan chupar a las viejas y a los maricones. Así que nos enmascaramos para embestir contra la impotencia que no nos permite otra salida de este pinche laberinto de padrotes, de pesos rotos, y de fantasmas de nuestro pasado glorioso y ensangrentado. Y a esa pochita –a quien me vi forzado a usar porque en esta vida, ya nos lo dijo Fuentes, los que no son chingones, pendejos son– cómo me gustaría envolverla de caricias aterciopeladas para protegerla de las bofetadas y el escupo que la madre patria de sus abuelos le proporcionará nomás por ser fruto de un vil acto histórico, progenitor de una cadena de actos de inmutable vileza multiplicada.

Qué jodidos, ya me vuelvo una paletita con el frío. ¿Cuánto tiempo necesitan para encontrar y destruir el sueño de un sólo pelado que menos cuenta que un grano de arena en este enorme hueco interrumpido apenas por una frágil vereda de acero –conexión entre dos círculos del infierno– por un tren destartalado y un pendejo mexicano aplastado entre ese tren y la noche oscura mientras unos hijos de puta buscan una cajita de mierda...?

¿Cómo, se habrán preguntado, sabe lo que en aquel momento pensó Lencho? La verdad es que este pasaje, por razones que después descubrirán, lo tuve que imaginar, o sea inventar. Ahora que saben esto, no faltará quién opine que he demostrado cierta tendencia acomodista al ponerlo en tan buena luz. Permítanme asegurarles que jamás dudé que sus inclinaciones machistas fueran irremediables y que, en efecto, sí lo motivaba un fuerte deseo de meterse en mis pantaletas. Sin embargo, siempre sentí una inexplicable necesidad de recordarlo de otra manera.

Quihubo, vida. ¿Te cansaste de esperar? Pasé por la librería y me dijeron que no estabas. Después, me detuve para comprar un disco. Mira, es el nuevo de Víctor Jara. Ven, cuéntame lo que hiciste hoy. ¿Yo? Pues tuve un día sumamente interesante. Primero, lo de siempre. Fui a mis clases, después a Casa Aztlán y ya sabes, horas y horas de plática. Después Luis y yo decidimos dar la vuelta al centro. Creo que estábamos un poco aburridos y salimos a ver qué onda. Del centro decidimos pasar a la Plaza de las Tres Culturas. ¿Te acuerdas que una vez te pedí que me llevaras y empezamos en esa dirección pero nunca llegamos? Nos topamos con algunos amigos tuyos y nos convidaron a tomar café y nunca fuimos. ¿Te acuerdas? Pues yo siempre quedé con ganas de ir y hoy fui con Luis.

Entramos a la capilla y fue allí donde ocurrió nuestra pequeña aventura. Yo estaba sentada, simplemente contemplando. Luis empezó a caminar, mirando todo con una intensidad perturbadora pero no le presté atención. Después de un rato lo vi ante el altar. Tú sabes cómo están esas piedras que forman el altar. Pues Luis empezó a tocarlas y a caminar de una a otra. Luego me di cuenta que las iba frotando como si fueran piedras preciosas. Entonces me puse a verlo desde donde yo estaba porque tuve la sensación de que algo no estaba bien. Fue entonces que empezó a restregarse contra las piedras y a llorar. Claro, yo me asusté y fui a donde estaba. Qué te pasa, y él que no me contestaba. Fue como si no me viera, y siguió así caminando de una piedra a otra como un loco, tratando de exprimirles no sé qué, y todo el tiempo llorando. Pues todo el mundo se puso a mirarlo y cuchichear, así que lo tomé de la mano y lo saqué de la capilla. Ya para entonces se estaba estremeciendo y gritando y llorando a baba suelta. Y yo, que este chavo se tomó algo –hongos o peyote o algo grueso. Ya sabes como siempre andamos con eso de que vamos a experimentar con hongos pero nunca lo hacemos. Pues no había manera de calmarlo y todo mundo mirando como bobos, algunos acercándose a ofrecer ayuda. Para entonces le daban así como convulsiones por todo el cuerpo y yo sin saber qué hacer, si llevarlo al hospital o qué.

Por fin logré sentarlo en un escalón allí en la plaza. Lo tomé en los brazos y empecé a mecerlo. Fue algo puramente instintivo, mecerlo, acariciarle la cara y los cabellos, arrullarlo como si fuera una criatura. Pues poco a poco se fue calmando y por fin se incorporó y dijo vámonos de aquí. Sin otra palabra caminamos varias cuadras. Sí, en silencio absoluto. Entramos en un pequeño bar y pedimos dos cervezas, y él sin decir palabra. Estuvimos así un largo rato y por fin dijo no sé qué onda hay en ese lugar, pero sentí unas vibraciones increíbles –una fuerza que me envolvía y me sofocaba. Luego empezó a desenvolverse una serie de visiones, de caras distorcionadas por dolor, de cuerpos en fuga, de sangre y de gritos. No sé, Mari, verdad que no sé qué me pasó allí. Jamás he tenido una experiencia así, pero fue tan real como el líquido en este vaso. Todavía estaba pálido y le temblaban las manos al llevar el cigarrillo a la boca.

Y tú sabes, Sergio, que Luis no es un muchacho escandaloso o frívolo. Es muy serio y retesensible, eso sí, quizá demasiado sensible. Pues la verdad es que me asusté. ¿Sergio, qué te pasa? ¿Por qué me has vuelto la espalda? Ay no, ahora tú. ¿Qué es esto? ¿Día de los niños chiflados? ¿Qué te pasa Sergio? Dime. ¿Qué te pasa querido? Por favor, Sergio dime, ¿qué te pasa? ¿Por qué estás llorando?

...Igual este momento a cualquier otro para preguntarte(me) por qué voy a México. Bueno lo de Steve resulta obvio pero eso de recuperar la niñez es pura bobada. La niñez no se recupera; ya pasó; puf, se borró; ya no existe. Lo que plasmó de bueno o de malo lo llevas atrapado dentro y eso es todo lo que existe –unas cuantas memorias y una bola de sentimientos, temores, esperanzas, prejuicios y actitudes contradictorias y ambivalentes que son precisamente tú. Así que vamos a darle por otro lado, ¿por qué vas a Mexicles?

Bueno, quizá sí haya algo de verdad en eso que vas a recobrar tu pasado, pero no tu pasado particular, sino una historia, o más bien una pre-historia, a la cual sigues atávicamente atada y que obsesivamente necesitas conocer. Regresar a la misma raíz, a la semilla, reandar los pasos perdidos para armarte con algo que te permita defenderte contra esa fuerza aluvial que te arrastra cada vez con más fuerza, amenazando arrancarte de tu misma esencia. Pero, de verdad, ¿qué tiene que ver tu realidad con México? Mira ustedes (bueno, nosotros) los neomexicanos, nuestras raíces hay que buscarlas en nuestra misma tierra.

Claro que los españoles sembraron en la Nueva México sus instituciones, su lengua, sus valores culturales, y son precisamente estos los que nos ligan al resto del mundo hispánico. Pero lo indígena hay que buscarlo en la misma tierra del Suroeste y en las culturas de esa región. Porque mismo como se desarrolló una cultura mestiza en México, se desarrolló otra en el valle del Río Grande, pero el ingrediente autóctono fue distinto al de México, al de Perú, o al de Bolivia. Mientras en México se desarrolló una nueva cultura mexicana, en tu tierra se dio la cultura neomexicana. Bueno, tienes, (o sea, tengo) y no tienes razón. Es verdad que podemos y

debemos hablar de una cultura distinta a la de México
en lo que atañe a la raíz indígena pero no hay que olvidar
tampoco que la raíz mexicana se extendió a través del
espacio y llegó a las colonias septentrionales primero con
los tlaxcaltecas que acompañaron a los primeros colonos
y que se establecieron en el barrio, o la vecindad, como
se decía y se sigue diciendo allá, de Analco en la Villa
de la Santa Fe, precisamente donde hoy se encuentra la
capilla de San Miguel.

Después aparecen nuevos retoños cuando la
Reconquista de De Vargas. ¿No es verdad que tu misma
familia descendió de un tal Juan de Soyago Sosa, nativo
de Texcoco, quien acompañó a De Vargas, junto con
su futura esposa, Ysabel Cabo Montezuma? Acuérdate
de cómo se les describe a los nuevos colonos que
acompañaron a De Vargas y a los descendientes de los
primeros colonos de la entrada de Oñate en los registros
oficiales traducidos en el libro de aquel sabio historiador:
algo de español (los capitanes, los frailes, los escribanos)
y mucho de mexicano. En otras palabras, *minha filha*,
la segunda oleada de colonos que a las riberas del Río
Grande arriba en 1692 traía sus agüitas enlodadas. Es
decir que en las venas de esos nuevos colonos, muchos
de ellos reclutados del Valle de México, fluía sangre
espesa de mestizaje; en algunos casos de uno y casi tres
cuartos siglos más de hanky panky entre las señoritas de
Tenochtitlán, dueñas de dulces y seductivos tipiles, y los
castizos pero no muy castos señores de Iberia.

Además, nuestra misma lengua revela ese mestizaje
cultural importado. ¿De dónde crees que vienen los muy
pintorescos giros, tecolote, guajolote, coyote, chapopote,
camote, elote –no Mingote no, mensa– cuate, chocolate,
pichicuate, esquite, mesquite, tequexquite, chíquete,
mecate, cajete, zacate, zoquete, jumate, aguacate,
cacahuate, nopal, tamal, comal, atole? Y disque el
dialecto de Nuevo México se caracteriza sobre todo por
sus arcaísmos castellanos. A ver, hagamos una pequeña
comparación cuantitativa: asina, mesmo, acual, vido,
vide, trujo, truje, trujimos, en pos de, ende, endenantes,
naidien, muncho, cuasi, anque, lección, escuro, curre,

lamber, jallar, jeder, jondo, juir, jueron, jumadera. Más o menos empate diría yo. Claro, has dado en el blanco: el mestizaje es una especie de empate. ¿Entonces por qué se habrán esmerado tanto en negar a uno de los equipos principales del partido tal como se ha hecho con tanto éxito en mi tierra?

Pero mira, chinita poblana, tampoco lo eres, así que no te hagas ilusiones, pochita, y hablando de ilusiones, no son éstos los arrabales, las afueras, los suburbios, los satélites, las villas de miseria del D.F.? ¡Alabado sea Dios, I have arrived in the motherland! ¿Cómo que the motherland? Yo creía que España era the true motherland of all manitos? Chale, querida, España is my fatherland...

¿Le ayudo con las maletas, señorita?

Es que buscaba a Lencho. Quería despedirme de él. ¿No lo ha visto usted?

Mire señorita, escúcheme bien. Sería mejor que no volviera usted a mencionar ese nombre y que olvidara que jamás conoció a ese joven.

Mi querida Mari,

Pasé a buscarte a Casa Aztlán y no te encontré, así que esta carta tendrá que ser mi despedida. Ahora mismo estoy en el aeropuerto y en treinta minutos salgo de este país por un período indeterminado. Quisiera poder decirte a dónde voy, pero por el momento ignoro mi destino. Sólo puedo decirte que anoche asesinaron a dos compañeros y por una pequeña coincidencia (lo que tú llamarías un milagrito) no me encontraba yo con ellos. Permanecer en México sin duda me costaría la vida, así que seguiré mi trabajo en otro sitio. Bien sabes que no faltan en este mundo hermanos y hermanas hambrientos de pan y justicia.

Mari, más que nada deseo estar contigo en este momento, mañana y siempre. Sin embargo hay cosas en la vida que tenemos que hacer, porque de otro modo nuestras vidas carecerían de significado. No sé decirte cuándo regresaré a México. Probablemente para entonces tú ya te habrás ido a tu tierra. Espero que en algún entonces podamos vernos otra vez. Mientras tanto me sostendrán en la lucha el sueño de un mundo humano y tu preciosa imagen.

Me acuerdo ahora que marchan obstinadamente en mi memoria los bellos momentos que pasamos juntos que nunca te conté lo de mi herida en la espalda. Entiende que todavía me duele tanto pensar en aquel horripilante e insensato episodio, que aun no puedo hablar de ello. No obstante, prometo contarte todo en nuestra próxima reunión.

Sergio

A veces
en sueños
todavía me voy
en el tren de la ausencia,
aferrada a ese boleto
que no tiene regreso.

On A Train
Called Absence

Biographical Note

Kay (Kayla) S. García, the co-translator of *On a Train Called Absence*, is a Professor of Spanish at Oregon State University. She is the author of *Broken Bars: New Perspectives from Mexican Women Writers* (University of New Mexico Press), and the translator of two novels by the Mexican author Brianda Domecq: *Eleven Days* (UNM Press) and *The Astonishing Story of the Saint of Cabora* (Bilingual Review Press). She has also translataed a collection of short stories by Brianda Domecq: *When I Was A Horse* (Texas Christian University Press). She has recently completed the translation of a novel by the Mexican author Jacobo Sefamí, *The Book of Mourners*, which will be published by Floricanto Press.

Kayla García was born in the United States and lived in Mexico for seven years and in Spain for two years. She has a Ph.D. in Spanish from the University of Wisconsin, Madison, as well as a B.A. and an M.A. in Spanish, and an M.A. in Latin American Studies.

Transformation and Betrayal: The Challenges of Translating *Paletitas de Guayaba*

by Kay (Kayla) S. García

A superficial perusal of *Paletitas de Guayaba* may give the mistaken impression that it is a simple text, relatively easy to read, analyze, and even to translate. However, a more careful reading reveals not only some techniques common to monolingual literature, such as the inclusion of epistolary, oneiric, and metaliterary elements, but also some more challenging characteristics sometimes present in Chicano literature, such as the utilization of multiple registers, dialects, and languages, all of which are intertwined and even juxtaposed by means of the complex processes of code switching or code mixing. In the field of sociolinguistics, the term *diglossia* (as introduced by Joshua Fishman) has been used to refer to the utilization of two different languages, or of two varieties of the same language, such as colloquial language and more formal language. Although the term diglossia is not commonly used to describe U.S. Latino Spanish, for the purposes of this article, I find it a useful tool to convey some of the complexities of Chicano dialects, as Fernando Peñalosa has done in his work *Chicano Sociolinguistics: a brief introduction* (41). Peñalosa describes a further distinction between *in-diglossia*, involving two closely related languages, and *out-diglossia*, involving two languages not closely related (41). This distinction leads us to the *complex diglossia* or *polyglossia* of Chicano Spanish, which may combine several varieties of colloquial and formal Spanish with colloquial and formal English, thus exhibiting characteristics of both in-diglossia and out-diglossia (Peñalosa 41-42). The choice of language or dialect regarding each word, phrase or sentence may depend on the context, and may reveal preferences based on social and cultural experiences. Individual speakers will have different educational and familial experience, and thus there is not a single, identifiable Chicano language, but rather a range of dialects that extend from primarily Spanish to primarily English, and a wide variety of ways in which individual elements are combined.

The challenges involved in translating Erlinda Gonzales-Berry's novel, therefore, were somewhat different from the challenges presented by more traditional, monolingual texts. *Traduttore, traditore,* to translate is to betray, according to the Italian dictum, so the question is always, what is betrayed? What is lost in translation? With poetry, one usually has to choose between mimicking the rhyme and rhythm of the original, or translating a more exact meaning. A similar choice is presented by the translation of a bilingual, bidialectal, and multi-registered text: Does one aspire to preserving the polyglossia per se, and thus in the case of *Paletitas de Guayaba* going from Chicano Spanish to Chicano English, or does one endeavor to make the text readily and fully accessible to monolingual readers?

My answer to this question is a deeply personal one, and as I answer it, I humbly acknowledge the right of any translator to make a different but equally valid choice. *Paletitas de Guayaba* already exists as a bilingual text, accessible in varying degrees to different readers, depending on their knowledge and experience of the Spanish and English languages and dialects, as well as U.S., Mexican, New Mexican and Chicano cultures. What I have attempted to do, with the help and encouragement of Erlinda Gonzales-Berry (who translated the text first, and then helped me with the re-translation), is to create a text that is accessible to monolingual readers of English, taking into consideration and trying to preserve the multiple registers present in the original (colloquial,

formal, academic, literary). Thus, I have translated the
text primarily into English, while inserting or retaining
a few, relatively familiar Spanish words as well as some
less familiar words that can be understood in context,
in order to maintain a bilingual "flavor," or at least a
hint of bilingualism. The result, of course, could not
be considered "Chicano English," since the few Spanish
words used would not necessarily be natural choices
for a speaker of Chicano English, and thus, inevitably,
something is lost in translation. Nevertheless, this
decision seems to be particularly appropriate as we
prepare for a bilingual edition of the novel, since
the original text will be readily available to bilingual
readers. However, let me clarify that my motivation for
translating literature is not so that people don't have to
learn Spanish, but rather, I translate in order to inspire
people to learn Spanish. It is my hope that by making
certain literary and cultural texts available to English
speakers, they will become more familiar with the
Chicano and Latin American culture and peoples, and
will thus find motivation to study Spanish, and to interact
with Spanish-speaking people within and without our
national borders.

Another challenge presented by this translation is
the necessity to preserve, honor and respect the "other,"
and to avoid transforming alterity into similarity. In
other words, if something is lost, that loss must be
reduced or compensated for as much as possible. I
must admit at this point that in spite of my extensive
experience living in Mexico, my Spanish surname, and
my present-day residence within the United States, I
cannot lay claim to being a Chicana. This admission
is based not only on bloodlines, but also on the lack of
first-hand experience on my part of the discrimination so
eloquently described in Erlinda Gonzales-Berry's novel.
In Paul St.-Pierre's article, "Translation: Constructing
Identity out of Alterity," he states that to translate a
text is to transform it, and then he poses the questions:
"What sort of transformation does the other undergo?
Is alterity recognized and maintained?" (8)   St.-Pierre

describes the dilemma facing translators in this way: "To translate [...] means to situate oneself in terms of another defined as "other" and the way in which such a relation is realized can run the gamut from complete denial of the alterity of the culture translated to slavish imitation" (4). As I translated this text, I was very conscious of this dilemma, and constantly endeavored to translate without erasing the difference presented by the "other." My success or failure in this respect may be measured by individual readers according to their own experience; but more importantly, the author herself, as part of the translation process, was allowed to disavow or re-translate any passage that did not ring true to her original intention. In this respect, I felt that I was truly privileged, and I have to recognize that other translators, working with authors who are not accessible, would have to struggle with this dilemma far more than I did.

Another aspect of the literary translator's task is the degree of freedom allowed. How closely does the translator follow the original text? Where and to what degree is it permissible to do a little literary creation of one's own in order to preserve the full meaning of the text, including word play, multiple connotations, irony, pace, and rhythm? In her article "The Role of Bilingualism in Translation Activity," Burce Kaya, borrowing from Uriel Weinrich's work *Languages in contact: findings and problems*, distinguishes between the "compound bilingual" (one who has learned two languages simultaneously) and the "co-ordinate bilingual" (one who has learned a second language at a later time, or in a different context), and she specifies that a "co-ordinate bilingual" produces a more independent translation: "A co-ordinate bilingual would have a different network of meanings of concepts, so his/her systems of languages are more independent from one another when compared to the relationship between the compound bilingual's language pairs" (5). With the translation that I have done of *Paletitas de Guayaba*, as a co-ordinate bilingual, I have attempted to create a new version of the text, a re-telling of the story that creates new meaning while it preserves as much of the original meaning as possible. Thus, the translation is similar to oral literature, which is flexible in its re-telling, rather than having the fixed meaning of a written text.

An example of this flexibility may be found in the translation of the title. The exact translation of the original title would be *Guava Popsicles*, which is a reference to the frozen fruit-flavored delights sold on the streets of Mexico. For someone who has lived in that country, the Spanish title evokes the sensory pleasures of Mexico, and stimulates a complex series of memories that may be culinary, tactile, auditory, or emotional, with the end result being a feeling of profound nostalgia. Unfortunately, "Guava Popsicles" does not have the same ring to it as "Paletitas de Guayaba," perhaps because of the number of syllables and the rhythm of the words, and/or because the guava is not a well-known fruit in the U.S. In order to preserve a feeling of nostalgia, the title in English has been rendered *On a Train Called Absence*, which references the Mexican song quoted at the beginning of the book. This title alludes to the metaphor of the train ride as a search for identity, and the name of the train, *Absence*, hints at a similar feeling as that evoked by the title in Spanish. Marc Zimmerman's work, *U.S. Latin Literature*, mentions Juan Bruce-Novoa's discussion of the theme of the loss of a world in Chicano literature, and the effort to recuperate the lost world through some kind of creative recreation of space (23). The title *On a Train Called Absence* brings up an absence, a void, the lost world to which there is no return. This is one of the premises of the novel, that one can not return to Mexico, or if you go to Mexico, you can not come back, and thus, one lives in perpetual exile, on an eternal train called Absence. A more literal interpretation would be that whether you are living in Mexico or the U.S., there will always be something missing. It was the profound nostalgia of a life in exile that first connected me to this text and made it possible for me to translate it in a way that goes beyond all the abovementioned terminology, and defies analysis.

Bibliography

Fishman, Joshua. "Bilingualism with and without diglossia; diglossia with and without bilingualism." *Journal of Social Issues* 23:29-38, 1967.

Kaya, Burce. "The Role of Bilingualism in Translation Activity." *Translation Journal.* January, 2007. http://accurapid.com/journal/39bilingual.htm

Peñalosa, Fernando. *Chicano Sociolinguistics: a brief introduction.* Rowley, Massachusetts: Newbury House Publishers, 1980.

St-Pierre, Paul. "Translation: Constructing Identity out of Alterity." HISTAL , January 2004.
http://www.histal.umontreal.ca/espanol/documentos/translation_constructing_identit.htm

Weinreich, Uriel. *Languages in contact: findings and problems.* The Hague: Mounton, 1953.

Zimmerman, Marc. *U.S. Latino Literature: An Essay and Annotated Bibliography.* Chicago: MARCH/Abrazo Press, 1992.

On A Train Called Absence

a novel by

Erlinda Gonzales-Berry

Translated from Spanish by

Kay (Kayla) S. García
and
Erlinda Gonzales-Berry

For Maya

Erlinda Gonzales-Berry

On a train called absence
I leave
My ticket is
one-way only
(Mexican song)

If ever you've thought
of changing your fate
think for a moment
who made you a woman
(Mexican song)

CHICANA WOMAN
break
into furious ecstasy
create
the mythical bonds
yourself
(Margarita Cota-Cárdenas)

This book is a work of fiction. Any similarities to real people, living or dead, are a result of mere coincidence.

The Desert

December 12th

I promised when it was over that I would not allow myself to think about you ever again. But what am I supposed to do? Here I am riding a decrepit train, embarking on a great adventure that is supposed to obliterate once and for all the smell of your flesh, feel of your touch, and sound of your voice, all of which still overwhelm my senses. Meanwhile, all I can do is smoke these disgusting cigarettes and mull over every lie, contradiction, and flimflamery that ever came my way. So of course I'm thinking about you.

The details of our story are still fresh in my mind as I set out on my solitary voyage, and while the distance between us increases with every click-click of the train's wheels, I begin to ponder how and why it failed. I must admit that I admire the subtlety with which you enmeshed me in a world of fantasy, the finesse with which you promised me the moon, the gentleness with which you offered to free me from the weight of twenty-three years of cultural baggage and the suffocating burden of my virginity. With what dexterity you assuaged my fears, removing one by one the cumbersome veils that covered my body, untangling the knotty mess of fibers that sheathed each and every one of my repressed desires. You took me by the hand and led me through dense forests of guilt and shame; the darkest corner of my unconscious was filled with your gilded light. Our bodies are the shore, nay they are the sea, they are a vast playground you said to me. Be a child once again you urged, and like a child I gave myself to your game. In an erotic trance I overcame the banal limitations of an existence held in check by admonitions of hellfire and brimstone. Like a child I succumbed to the pleasure of running on the beach, of plunging my body into the ocean waters. Your name is beauty you said to me; your childish laughter enchants me. I adore your preening and prancing like a young mountain goat, but see that bridge? We must cross it now, for I am a man who desires a woman. I can't be your father forever. Beneath that olive-toned skin of yours lies another world. Once again you took me by the hand and led me into a world of blazing passion. As was natural I became frightened. But soon I realized that these were not the fires of hell into which I had stumbled. The raging flame rose from my very being and in each circle of this inferno I discovered greater degrees of pleasure. Your name is beauty you said; if you could see yourself you'd be amazed: your playful feline eyes have become the eyes of a tigress —in heat?, I asked.

My words fell heavily upon your ears. Ice replaced your searing flame, your golden thighs turned metalic blue. That cannot be, you said. And I, but it must. See that gate? You must open it now. As you taught me the formulas of economics, as you revealed the path to sea and shore, you must unlock for me the gate to maternity.

In disbelief you said to yourself, I should have known for I was warned. Beware of girls with skin the color of olives. One faulty step and they will devour you. Theirs is a primitive instinct. True, they will deliver unto you the most occult of pleasures but at the very moment when you surrender your senses, when you find yourself immobilized by their seething passion, they will bury their fangs deep into your jugular demanding respect, family and home. So secure in my game, the indisputable champion of the pas de deux, I said worry not to my friends. Had there not been countless students that I introduced not only to the world of economics but also to Eros' own domain? And had they not one by one at the end of their apprenticeships shown effusive gratitude? Had the lessons of their first master not prepared them to sally forth into the world?

Careful dear friend, they admonished. You don't

know those dark-skinned girls. Unlike us they do not see life as a blank page upon which to draw with steady hand and eye of hawk the shape of our own destinies, nor do they chisel their concrete reality according to their own projected plan. Their way is to surrender to life's experience, to a primordial instinct that at the propitious moment signals: THIS IS THE ONE. No, you said, this cannot be. You are not part of the plan drawn up long ago by my own hand. Notwithstanding the sweetness of your flesh, I cannot accede. You have no land, no name, no connections. (These were not your words but those spoken to me by my intuition.) Be gone from me you olive-skinned cat-eyed creature. Go explore the world for it is not yet time to open that gate, the key to which I am not the sole proprietor.

My mistake was to confuse pleasure with love, is that not so? I cared so much for you; I offered the most precious gift I had to give, and you refused to accept it. And now all the pleasure we shared has turned to bile and I am consumed by shame and guilt. But you know something, I did learn a thing or two from this experience. You men of golden manes think you own the world. You think you're God Almighty. The world is yours and you do and undo according to your divine plan. And human beings are also yours to manipulate as you see fit. Feelings, emotions, they aren't worth a fig, are they? They too must be governed by calculated reason and a utilitarian view of the world. So my dear master, my gratitude is less than nothing; in fact, I spit in your face. Does my candor surprise you? The truth is (and do forgive the need I have to humiliate you, to flog you with the truth) I doubt you have the sensibility to appreciate the fact that innocence is a condition that easily gives way to bitterness and spite.

My sole consolation is the certainty that some day when all that surrounds you loses its flavor, you will recall the very moment in your life when you disdained the salt of the earth.

I don't know why I bothered to write this letter. Perhaps to place in perspective our relationship and begin to patch the tears in this vessel from which my emotions and my sentiments gush like the raging waters of a storm unleashed by heaven's own fury-bound gods. Amen.

xxx

P.S. Please, do not respond. I want mine to be the last word said regarding this chapter of my life.

The tremulous beam of the ancient and decrepit train penetrated the dark reaches of the night and slowly but inexorably devoured the barren miles on its long journey to the macrocephalic city. The clickety-clack of steel on steel kept her awake. She sat in her berth, rested her back on a pillow, lit one cigarette then another, and began to write in her notebook:

...For God's sake why do I do this to myself? Don't I care that someday the ogre of lung cancer will get me? They'll find those little air sacks lined with charcoal, rotten, burned to a crisp, a foul mess, when they perform an autopsy. Papá is absolutely right. What a filthy habit! Oh well, what can I do? This addiction is incurable and I am incorrigible. Perhaps I'll be able to stop once I get there; I can replace it with tequila and Tecate —and *limón*. I wonder why it is that lime always reminds me of my childhood? Not my childhood back there, but my *other* childhood, in the place where I'm headed right now, in México: México, Jalisco, Guadalajara, Simón Bolívar Street, Señora Jaramillo's apartments. Apartments for Gringos. That's what they were, apartments for Gringos, except for us. We weren't Gringos although it's true that we lived there. In a way we were, well not exactly Gringos (my God, how can you even entertain that idea?). What I mean is from the United States. No way to deny that. Even though we spoke Spanish and were dark skinned we were from "the other side." No way getting around that. And Papá's friends, or rather his coworkers from the AFTOSA[2], were all Anglos. But I tried like hell to act Mexican, imitating the intonation of my Mexican friends like a parrot. And who might those Gringos be that visit your home they would ask and I was quick to respond *no sé*. I don't know them and I could care less. You're from

2   Mexican-American Commission for the Eradication of Foot-and-Mouth Disease (*fiebre aftosa*).

up there aren't you? No way. We're from here. My father has a few acquaintances because of his job, *sabes*.

And my older sister –damn her anyway– was a friggin' Pocha. She hung out all the time with those disgusting white girls from Texas. I could never understand why she got involved with them. Perhaps at her age she couldn't shed her identity. It was too late for her to become a Mexican. Boy, not me. I dreamed every night about being reborn as a Mexican. BORN AGAIN MEXICAN. That was what I wanted to be. When my sister and the two Gringas from Texas left school without permission, I pretended not to know them. Hey, isn't that your sister, the one that Mees Beti is dragging across the playground? RELEASE THEM, LET THEM GO HOME IF THAT'S WHAT THEY WANT! (shouted the principal through the loudspeaker).

Damn her and all of her high-falutin' gringa airs. There I was standing in line with all the other kids from the American School, saluting the Mexican flag and dying of shame when my sister bolted because she was who she was, and didn't want to –or should I say wasn't able to– be reborn Mexican. I sure played the Judas. No, that's not her. Looks like her, doesn't it? But no, that's definitely not my sister. And later my folks came to pick me up. No you can't stay. There's no way we're leaving you here with these tyrants. It's the nuns' school for you. And I clung like a barnacle to Mees Mary, screaming and blubbering like a baby as I buried my face in her consoling bosom.

My theatrics were in vain, because I was promptly deposited in the care of the nuns. Those old biddies went out of their way to make my life miserable. There I was, a true Leo, seeking human warmth like a cat searching for the maternal love I had known in Mees Mary's enormous tits. What a rude awakening! My new caretakers were walking icebergs dressed in black, locked behind walls that were topped off by jagged pieces of broken bottles. Those delicate saints, precious mothers and wives of Christ. Mothers from hell, that's what they were. Colder and more dreadful than salt water in a corn field. It was then and there that this impressionable child began her days of suffering, most of which have mercifully vanished from her memory.

Unfortunately I can't say the same about my dreams. From time to time the sweet little nuns with their hooded heads and angel faces distorted as if filtered through a wide-angle lens find their way into my dreams. Right there in my very private dreams they form a circle around me and begin pushing me from gloved hand to gloved hand and they keep pushing me until I fall over crying, screaming and calling out for Mees Mary. *Gracias a Dios* that ordeal lasted only two months because if it had lasted any longer, I would have changed my status of Born Again Mexican. The truth is I learned to hate those nuns and because of them I almost came to hate all Mexicans. But I was spared that fate, since I was removed from there in the nick of time, just before renouncing forever my adopted country. And look at me now: fifteen years later on a glorious journey bent on finding once again the perfume of bougainvillea, the exquisite music of Mexican Spanish, the pungent smell of lime, a cup of chocolate with cinnamon, a delectable guava popsicle, Lake Chapala, the patio in the old house at Sayula, human warmth...

Do you remember, Sergio, the day we met? I was waiting for Julie in front of the bookstore. It was just starting to rain and you invited me to wait indoors. Pssssst, come on in, you're going to get wet, you said to me and no sooner had I entered than you asked me if I was a Chicana. How did you know? Don't tell me that my clothes or my walk gave me away. That's not what you said that day; as a matter of fact what you did say was you've got it written on your forehead. And I answered that I might be from the other side but under no circumstances was I a Chicana, and quite frankly I didn't care for that label since where I came from people thought Chicanos were a bunch of Communist rabble-rousing opportunists. Oh, so you don't like *comunistas*, you said with an amused twinkle in your eye. Then you must be from New Mexico. According to my sources New Mexicans are quite conservative and don't feel allied to the rest of *la gente chicana*. What the hell do I know about politics?, I replied; for the moment my most pressing concern is how to survive in this damn jungle.

When I told you I was studying at the North American Center, you countered that no wonder I was so disillusioned, since people there were a pack of reactionaries whose only interest was accumulating Gringo dollars. Then I told you about how miserable I was there; I had come to Mexico to meet Mexicans and the only students at the *Centro* were foreigners who barely spoke Spanish. What's worse, in spite of having no problem understanding the language and even speaking it fairly well, I had been stuck in a beginners' class, supposedly to rid me of my Pocho accent. Afterwards I told you that when I arrived they didn't have a host family for me and I had to stay at the director's house, where I overheard the secretary tell someone that they didn't have a family for me because their families didn't like to host Pochos. Can you imagine how much it hurt to learn that Mexicans like Gringos more than Chicanos? That's when I told Santiago, the director, that if they didn't find me a home *inmediatamente*, I was going to demand my money back and get the hell out of there, and they would never see another Pocha or Pocho in their friggin' school again. That's how I ended up living with Julie and the Córdova family.

When Julie entered the bookstore, you chuckled and commented that my trip to Mexico wouldn't be a complete waste, since at least I would learn to coexist with Gringos. Isn't it ironic that over there we can't stand the sight of each other and here lady luck deals me a Gringa roommate? Nothing like living with the object of our prejudice in order to learn that it is our basic *humanidad* that unites us all (and some perverse element of that humanity that separates us).

And by the way, tell Carlos that if he treats Julie like a dirty dishrag, I will strangle him with my very own hands. Isn't that a kick? All my life I've loathed *güeras* and here I am defending one like a champ. The truth is that Julie is cool and I like her, but *pobrecita*, your fellow countrymen won't leave her alone for one damn minute. I truly hope Carlos doesn't turn out like most of these jerks who see her as easy prey and wham bam thank you ma'am, because Julie just isn't like that. Yes I know, you already explained the bit about the colonized mentality of Mexican males and how after so many centuries of domination they've assimilated a warped mentality, lusting after the master's property because it's the only way to get back at him. Mexican males don't even begin to understand what motivates their behavior, but there you have them drooling over every blond that sets foot on this *tierra sagrada,* you said in all seriousness. I had never thought of it in those terms, I replied; I thought they did it just to prove they're machos. How could you have thought of it in those terms, if you don't like politics?, you retorted. So listen up, —what's your name?— okay, Marina, our lives are political, you said, and if they aren't they should be and you should be a Chicana. It's your moral responsibility to learn about the Chicano Movement. Then you pulled out a bunch of articles and Acuña's book and you told me to read them and then afterwards we'd see whether or not I was a Chicana. You also promised to introduce me to your Chicano friends at Casa Aztlán.

During that whole week I did nothing but read. I ditched my classes at the Center and I even forgot how pissed off I was about how Mexicans reject their kinfolk from the other side. Of course with each passing day I began to understand the resentment they feel toward those who leave in search of the proverbial El Dorado. I realized that their historical wounds (which are ours, as well) are so deep that it is only natural for them to hate the ones who leave.

You know what I'd like to do, Sergio? I'd like to do a survey on attitudes of Mexicans toward Chicanos. What do you think? I could include opinions about culture, politics, and language, as well as sources of information, media influence, etc. What really interests me is that whole bit about how Mexicans feel about our language because I just get so exasperated. I don't know why you can't give us credit for something. For more than a century and a half we've lived under the glorious Stars and Stripes, with English the dominant and prestigious language, while everything under the sun was being done to eliminate Spanish. But in spite of everything, we cling to our language, even though it's *machacado*, as you say here, all mashed to hell. What's important is that we feel that it belongs to us and we hang on to it with pride. What you don't understand is that Spanish is a stigmatized language in the United States because the people who speak it are stigmatized, second-class citizens. The Gringos belittle our culture and our language; they treat us like *pinches animales*. It's hard to believe, but there were once signs in restaurants and swimming pools in the Southwest that read:

NO DOGS
NEGROES
MEXICANS

Nevertheless, they didn't wipe us out completely,
didn't shove us into ovens, because they needed our
strong backs and our willingness to work for pennies. We
have to force ourselves to learn English because that's the
only way to defend ourselves and of course our Spanish
is going to suffer in the process, but that doesn't mean
we're going to let it go. Even though they have refused
to teach it to us in school; even though we're illiterate in
the language we suckled at our mamas' breast, we cling
to our mother tongue and insist on our right to speak
it, in defiance of the official language. And all you and
your fellow citizens can say is, God save us from those
barbarous Pochos, they shouldn't even speak it at all.

Do you understand what I'm trying to tell you?
What do you mean keep quiet for a minute? *Ay*, Sergio,
don't you see how important it is for me to speak about
this? But there's one thing you don't ever tire of, right?
Whoever baptized you all Latin Lobers knew exactly
what she was talking about. No, I'm not trying to reduce
you to a stereotype —I'm just trying to inflate your
ego, well, and that too. Of course I like it; how could
I not like it when you know exactly how to please me.
Mmmmmmmmmmm. There. No. No. Up a bit. There.
Perfecto. No, not so hard....*Así. Sí. Sí, Síííííí*, Sergio. Oh
baby, my sweet, sweet lover, who else could I possibly
belong to, if not to you? If you want proof, kill me,
right now. *SÍ, ¡MÁTAME PERO NO ME DEJES! (Go
ahead, kill me, but don't leave me!)*, I holler, in my best
melodramatic Lola Beltrán voice.

What do you mean I'm a shameful hussy? And loony
too? Well, yeah, I am a bit daffy as my mamá would say
(oh dear, and what would she say if she saw me now, good
God!). Crazy for you and crazy in love, just like you, right,
sweetheart? Well if not crazy in love, at least you could
admit that carnal desire has driven you totally gaga, for
if that weren't the case, you would have told me to get

lost because you're up to here with all my issues. But you
understand, don't you Sergio, this obsessive need I have
to vent all my frustrations, my doubts, my outrage, and
even my dreams, in short, to create some order in my
world and connect with someone that understands me.
And that someone is you my dear, dear Sergio.

..What should I do? Should I write to him, or not? I've got it planned word for word in my mind. But what good will it do to write him a letter? It's all over. He can go to hell if he feels so inclined. Take a flying fuck for all I care. Hasta la vista baby, that's what I said to him when it was over. *Fini. Caput-o.* Oh, right, and who the hell do I think I'm fooling? With my heart bleeding all over my sleeve I keep trying to tell myself I don't care. Who exactly am I trying to fool? But really, what happened? I just don't understand. I gave him every inch of myself and he rejected me. And what I desperately want now is to reach him, to write a bridge of words across the void that separates us. How many miles have I traveled? Five hundred, seven hundred? What difference does it make? With each mile his image and his presence just become stronger. Let's see, I could say something like this:*Here I am riding a decrepit train, embarking on a great adventure that is supposed to obliterate once and for all the smell of your flesh, feel of your touch, and sound of your voice, all of which still overwhelm my senses...*

lesbian

Sergio, you don't know how frightened I felt because you were late. Yes, I know you're here now, but that doesn't help me one bit when you leave the city. I know that you won't answer me but I am going to ask you again: Where did you go? What did you do? What do you mean you can't tell me? You don't trust me, right? No, I'm not trying to pick a fight. Come on, take off your shirt and I'll massage your back.

Yes, I spent the whole afternoon at Casa Aztlán, talking to Isaura. You know what?, I really like her. Remember when I first met her, I was afraid of her? When I went to bed at night I couldn't go to sleep because I was scared she would climb in the sack with me. And now I'm really embarrassed because I realize that my fears were a form of prejudice, just as bad as the racial prejudice I condemn so much. It all boils down to fear of the "other," don't you think?

Well, yes, I felt it from the first day you took me to Casa Aztlán. Don't you remember the pillow fight we had? Can you believe my welcome to Casa Aztlán was a barrage of pillows? I laughed so hard I cried, and in that moment of insane frivolity I knew I was with family. Before you took me there I was so disillusioned. I felt so defeated, all I wanted was to return to New Mexico. But when I met them, Toña, Manuel, Beto (what a bastard he can be sometimes, don't you think?) Lupe, Luis and Isaura, everything changed.

Do you remember how the fight began? I will never forget what Isaura said after that little tiff I had with Beto, who began to razz and insult me the minute I arrived, for being a *manita*. It's just that the few *manitos* that I've known –Beto shot at me– have always been a pain in the butt. They're so arrogant, they think they're *gachupines*, *Spaniards* and don't want to join our cause because supposedly they aren't Chicanos. And you got that come-on-Beto-I-told-you-guys-this-chick-needed-tender-love-and-care-and-here-you-go-with- your-shit look. What did I say to him? You're right, dear heart, I declared that I had always felt very Mexican because I had lived in Mexico when I was a child, but at that moment I felt very disillusioned after being rejected mercilessly by so many Mexicans. That's when Luis said, tell me about it girl, that's part of the collective experience of all the inhabitants of Casa Aztlán. Why do you think we're here together? Living here is like living in a Chicano barrio in the States. Casa Aztlán protects us from the hostile world out there. No, it wasn't Toña, but Lupe who intervened: it's true, one feels like that in the beginning but as you get used to things and your Spanish improves you begin to lose your fear and little by little you find your way and things seems less hostile, especially at the UNAM[3] because ideologically speaking they have no choice but to accept us there.

Is it true, Sergio, that your ideology forces you to care about me? I thought it was your biology, your reptilian cerebrum. You know, I've formed a new hypothesis about why tourists in Mexico act like immoral fools once they get here. Do you want to hear it? Well, first you will have to inspire me. Don't ask me, let's see what you can come up with on your own. Oooooooooh, love of my life, now, that's what I call divine inspiration.

Well, here's my idea: over there everything is so sterile, so whitewashed, so artificial that the reptile portion of their brain has become atrophied, in a collective evolutionary sense. Yes, they're all the same. When they come here the colors, smells, noises, looks only Mexicans can give that penetrate the very soul, all that overstimulation assails their senses and awakens their little reptile tail and they wag it like crazy, dancing on tables, shouting like *charros,* drinking *pulque* until they're numb, accompanying strangers to fifth-rate hotels, in short, acting as if there were no tomorrow and no hell either. It's a moment of insanity, of mental

3   National Autonomous University of Mexico, in Mexico City.

unbalance that one feels upon entering a world so vital and so distinct from one's own.

Understand? So it is, my little piece of heaven, that these delicious moments we spend together are the direct result of the over-ripe mangoes in the *mercado* that awakened my carnal appetite, encapsulated in a tiny salamander that slept here, look, right here at the base of my cranium, which upon awakening has become an enormous crocodile, devourer of slender and prodigiously endowed young men. Say that again. Did you really say what I think you said? That your lizard doesn't live at the base of your cranium, but between your thighs? *Ay, ingrato!* I spend the whole week waiting to share with you this incredible idea that my little chicken-brain concocted and all you can do is say foolish things like that. What else can I expect from a nice boy like you with a social conscience? So, say it. Okay, I'll forgive you this time and if you calm down your *lagartijo* a bit I'll tell you the rest of Isaura's story.

Let's see, where was I? Oh yes, Beto, *pinche* Beto got it into his head that he had to provoke me *sans cause juste*. Hey *manita,* let's go back to that bit about your feeling Chicana. Why don't I believe you? Experience tells me that reactionary *manito* ideology is impenetrable, indisputable and disgusting. That's what he said, right? Then I said all those wonderful things about you, remember? Let's see, I began like this: *újule mano,* first I had to prove to Mexicans that I'm a worthy person; now I have to prove it to you. I don't know what I would have done without Sergio. He is the only person that hasn't treated me like trash. Through his eyes (yes, through *teus olhos bellos, meu bem*) I am discovering and assimilating the deep wounds that afflict this country and its people. Through him I am beginning to understand what motivates them to reject us the way they do, but what's more important, through him I'm beginning to understand the history of my people, and that is what's so ironic about it all. I had to come to Mexico and meet Sergio in order to discover the Chicano movement.

Nevertheless, the young man of spiked tongue

continued to insult me. What do you mean, mine isn't exactly dull? All I said was he should stop hassling me, and perhaps he was needling me because of some *manita* who told him he was an impotent imbecile, and then Toña interrupted, Mari, don't get pissed. Can't you see that Beto is so passionate about *la causa chicana* that he sometimes can't control his rhetoric? But believe me, he has truly enlightened things to say regarding our identity, our history and the opportunities that at this very moment our *raza* must seize.

No, Sergio, what I said was: well then, I guess that means I should forgive him for being so rude. So, go ahead, Beto. There's nothing I would like more in this world than to listen to a nincompoop pontificate royal stupidities. It was THEN that Isaura —finally I get to Isaura's intervention— said: Come on Mari, I'll show you our bedroom. Afterwards you and Beto can sign a truce. Now it's up to us, the *belles dames* of Casa Aztlán, to give you some advice on how to survive this urban jungle filled with Mexican machos (present company excluded, perhaps) and a few Chicano *vatos locos* that could easily give lessons to the natives on how to insult, oppress, and reduce the second sex to mere cheesecake.

I loved what she said, and also Toña's little cheer: HIT 'EM AGAIN, HIT 'EM AGAIN, HARDER, HARDER, but Beto's retort caught me offguard: *újule*, Sergio, if you've got your eye on this Pochita, forget it because Isaura's already won her over with her lesbian harangue. That gave me the creeps. But now that I know her and have ceased fearing her, I care for her deeply and each day become more conscious of the triple monkey she carries on her back. And clearly, that knowledge tempers somewhat my sense of personal rage.

I told you, that's where our dog bit me when I stuck a straw in his ear. Papá got so furious he wanted to kill him but Mamá didn't let him. Spoiled, my ass, Sergio; my parents never spoiled me. In fact, you know what Mamá said? That I was a pesky troublemaker who was always tormenting Othello —I swear that was the dog's name. Can you believe it, my own mother defended a dog, *un perro, un chien,* and dismissed me as a nuisance. How can I avoid being plagued by all kinds of Freudian complexes? You tell me, love. Five years old. Of course it hurt. Well kiss it if you want but the truth is it doesn't hurt anymore. And how about that scar on your back, what happened to you? Oh, so some lazy afternoon when you're in a mood for talking, you'll tell me? I can see that day coming: I'll be a little eighty-year-old lady; tell me, don Sergio, what happened to you there where you have that scar on your back? (Howling laughter).

Well, you know it was that day at Casa Aztlán that I fell in love with you. Wait, let me get the story straight. When Beto insulted Isaura, she and Toña began to throw pillows at the guys. Then they armed themselves and the feather-filled projectiles flew in all directions. We all jumped in except you, who just sat there watching us. What do you mean you saw it as an exclusive Chicano celebration? Really? Something of an initiation ritual for me? How funny, I never thought of it that way. Well anyway, after we all fell in a pile on the floor I was overcome by this strange sense of ambivalence; on one hand I wanted to remain there absorbing the intimacy offered by my new friends, actually my new family, and on the other, when I looked in your direction sitting there alone and left out (and no doubt about it, my great weakness is solitary and melancholic males) I felt this incredible desire to embrace you, to kiss your eyelids, your beautifully chiseled cheekbones (vestige of the ancient peoples of this land, I thought to myself), and your thin, sensitive lips behind which lingered unspoken desires that materialized as they escaped through your eyes and shamelessly made their way in my direction. Yes, it was at that very moment when I felt so close to my Chicano friends that I felt the first impulse to lie down beside you. I think that is the kind of person that I am, that is my nature. At the very moment when I am about to identify myself totally and wholeheartedly with something, a part of me holds back and flees in the opposite direction. Of course the upshot is a certain tendency toward schizophrenia, well if not schizophrenia clinically speaking, then perhaps neurosis.

And there you have it. That was the afternoon when I fell in love with you and to prove the authenticity of my statement I will, at this very moment, offer you the gift most highly desired by men in every corner of the world:

Oh, ecstasy! Visit this handsome young man and make him a slave to this conversant instrument without which it would be impossible to lie about one's neighbor, confess iniquities and sins, sing corridos, say aaaaah when so ordered by the doctor, or take a lingering, blissful taste of a luscious guava-flavored popsicle....

Ay, Dios, How can these people live in this godforsaken desert? Sand, sand, and more sand; here and there a shanty shaken by voracious winds. Dear Lord, what do they eat? This earth was not meant to produce a single mouthful of food. Not a solitary village to be seen in this endless emptiness. Nonetheless, hunched figures appear occasionally like ghosts walking along the track. Where are they headed? There's nothing here. An infinite void. Barren solitude. A landscape never designed to sustain human life. But there goes another man and his beast of burden, dark silhouettes against the blazing sunrise. What difference can there be? Tell me, God, since you created that man in your image, and that beast, and this limitless space, and the majestic dawn: What's the difference between that man's life, and the life of his beast?...

I didn't hear you come in. I was asleep, and dreaming. Wait a minute, it's coming back to me. My grandmother, yes, I was dreaming about my *abuelita*. She was making me an outfit, a lacey blouse and a yellow skirt, as she did when I was a child living with her. She always made me clothes. She would cut up her old dresses and remake them in my size. Then she'd say, come try it on. When she saw me in the new dress her face would light up with pleasure. Now, let me fix your hair. She'd comb my hair and put a touch of makeup on my face. She was really my great aunt, not my grandmother. She was my papá's aunt but since she never had any children of her own she asked her sister —yes the one that married her cousin— to let Papá live with her, so she was like a mother to him. That's why on Papá's side of the family we had two *abuelas,* one grandmother and the other a great aunt whom we also called *abuela*. When I was ten years old she asked Papá to let me live with her because my grandpa worked on a ranch and came to town only on weekends and she was terribly lonely. At first it was really strange. I was used to my sisters and all the noise and chaos that reigned at home. At Grandma's everything was always in its place and words were spoken almost in a whisper. At home everyone talked at the same time and squealed and hollered and it was always a carnival. But at my grandmother's house everything was different.

After dressing and primping me, she would ask if I didn't want to visit Mamá because she had a headache and wanted to sleep a while. So I would trot off happy as a lark with my white lace gloves and my *abuelita's* beaded purse. When I got to my parent's house my sisters were always doing housework, washing dishes, cleaning the floor, ironing, sweeping the yard. As I made my royal entrance, a regular little princess, they'd look at me with an oh-its-that-disgusting-creep kind of look and they'd barely talk to me. I would stay by Mamá and I could hear them giggling and talking about me behind my back. When she wasn't looking, they would gang up on me and pinch me and pull my hair. When I finally got back to Grandma's I'd be a mess, my hair flying out in all directions and my new dress torn and muddied. And every chance I got, I'd visit them again with hopes that this time they would treat me well and play with me, but my hopes were always dashed. After a couple of years I returned to live at home and we all forgot about our differences. In fact, they took me back as if nothing had ever happened. I think that experience deeply affected my personality. For a while I used it as a pretext for manipulating my parents. I'd throw in their faces the fact that they didn't love me, so they gave me away to Grandma like a little orphan. But the truth is that I was so happy to be back where there were signs of life that I soon forgave them. Sometimes my sisters and I remember and they call me Little Princess and I call them Cinderellas and we all laugh about it.

Well, my *abuelita* died last year. Oh Sergio, it was the most awful and dehumanizing thing you could imagine. After the operation they connected her to all these machines. She was like that for ten days with tubes in her mouth, up her nose, and in every other orifice. Her skin was yellow and covered with bruises. She never opened her eyes and we didn't know if she was conscious or not and those damn machines kept forcing her to breathe. Mamá and Papá got really upset, as you can imagine, seeing her like that. Papá was beside himself because he had made the decision to go ahead with the operation. Otherwise, she would have died within a couple of hours, but because they operated she was stuck living in that mechanized hell, a prisoner of those bleeping machines, and of course he felt guilty.

While we were at the hospital, we got to know another family; my sister already knew them because they were from her village. Their eighteen-year-old son had been in a motorcycle accident in front of their home on his graduation day and he, too, was like a vegetable hooked up to machines. They had a huge family: ten sons and daughters, their spouses, their children, as well as the elders. For ten days they camped out at the hospital. They would make beds on the floor in the hallway and sleep there; they brought food and just moved right in. And every hour a couple of members of each family were allowed to see their patient for a few minutes.The young graduate and Grandma were in the same condition: they didn't move, didn't speak, didn't open their eyes. All you could hear was the hissing of the respirator. Whoever went in just stood there staring without knowing what to do. Finally Papá couldn't stand it any more and he refused to see Grandma because it upset him so much. So Mamá, my sisters and I took turns.

The tenth night I went in with my sister, the one who became a holy-roller several years ago. It's hard for me to accept that every aspect of her life is controlled by her religion. The worst of it is that she really believes that women must blindly obey their husbands, because the bible tells her so. Just before going in, we had all been talking and agreed that it was absurd for them to keep Grandma alive on those obnoxious machines. What she really deserved was to die with dignity in her own home. The doctors kept insisting that it was their moral responsibility to keep her hooked up, as long as three vital organs were functioning.

That night it was about eleven when my sister and I went in to check on her, as we'd been doing for ten days in a row. Since it was the first time I went in with Luz, I was shocked when she began to talk to Grandma. Other members of the family didn't say anything; they just stood there staring at her, weeping and sniffling. But Luz immediately began to talk to her in a completely natural tone. She told her God was waiting for her with open arms, it was time for her soul to return to him, she shouldn't resist his will, heaven was quite lovely, there were gardens and orchards all over, Grandpa was waiting for her, and on and on. And Grandma just lay there motionless, without giving any sign of being able to hear or understand. Then all of a sudden, the strangest thing happened. As my sister continued to speak, gently caressing Granny's forehead, the numbers on the pulse machine began to change. When we walked in it was at 140. Then it started to drop: 135-134-130. As her pulse dropped, mine started to race and I could scarcely breathe. I had never seen anyone die, and I felt as if death were right there beside us, personified, with a big grin and inscrutable eyes. When the machine registered 94, it stopped dropping but the respirator continued to hiss. Just then the nurse entered and told us it was time to leave. As we huddled in the hallway, Luz was the very portrait of serenity, but I was on the verge of hysteria. When she put both arms around me, I felt a calm wave spread throughout my body. We were standing there holding each other when the nurse approached to inform us that Grandma had died.

That night's experience will forever be engraved in my memory. In fact, I am haunted by that whole traumatic episode of Grandma's death: the horror of the machines, the frustration caused by seeing her like that, neither alive nor dead, for such a long time. Sometimes I forget it for a short while but today I remembered again. I imagine she wants me to pray for her and that's why I dreamed about her. That's what they say when you dream about the dead, isn't it?

The boy who crashed on his motorcycle? He died that same night, at twelve o'clock.

Let's see. I'll have a slice of papaya, a cup of coffee with cream and some *molletes*. That's all. No, wait a moment. Do you have any cigarettes? It doesn't really matter, so long as they burn, produce smoke and cancer, and I won't have to wait until the next stop. You're right. That's exactly what my father tells me. Well, what can I do? I'm an incurable addict.

...And you, dirty old man, what are you gawking at? Doesn't your wife have legs, and breasts? The poor thing. And on my right, there's another one. At least this guy wipes the drool with his napkin. And his wife must be blind. If I were that lady, I'd bop him on the bean: Take this you swine, you shameless lech, stop undressing that girl with your eyes, and eat your breakfast...

No, I don't need anything. Really I don't. How much longer? Did you say there's a stop in Durango? No, I feel fine, it's just that I'm tired. I didn't sleep much last night.

...Damn these pesky porters, they keep hassling me. Just because I'm from over there they think I'll jump in bed with them like some shameless Gringa. I think that's why I didn't sleep last night. I was scared to death that one of them would sneak into my berth. But really, deep down, I'm not afraid. Not like over there where one can get attacked in the middle of the street in broad daylight, and everyone just stands around gawking like fools. Mamá and Papá have told me all these horror stories about Mexicans. As if they were any different. I think the problem is that over there we've somehow come to believe that we're superior to them. Especially in New Mexico, where people don't like to be called Mexican. I'm not *Mexican*, I'm *Spanish* they tell you right off. I tell Mamá and Papá, can't you see that we have the same origins, and we're related? Don't tell me we're different because we're separated by some abstract border, by worthless colored pieces of cloth? Those are ideas that Americans (my folks forbid us to use the word *Gringos* in front of them) have made us believe. No, *hija*. They're *surumatos*. They're violent and untrustworthy. They come here and take our jobs (not to mention *las güisas* they take from the guys). No way.

That's how my parents and so many others think. Thank God I don't have those complexes. I defend Mexico as if it were my own homeland. Actually it is my homeland, the one I adopted when I was a child; that's why I'm returning now, to reclaim my lost paradise. My parents don't feel the love that I feel for Mexico. I can't blame them since they were born over there.

Their parents and grandparents were also born in the United States, not because they chose to but because that was the historical reality that fate assigned them. I am certain, nonetheless, that the generations before them felt something for Mexico. Even though they were not born in what is politically defined as Mexico, I am certain that they carried it in their collective unconscious and that it flowed in their veins. The proof lies in the fact that in our native language, in Spanish, we have always called ourselves *mexicanos*. We only refer to ourselves as *Spanish* when we're speaking English; I suppose it's to impress the AMERICANOS. In fact, we'll even do handsprings if we think that will please them. What damn fools we are. Because the truth of the matter is that nothing we do pleases them. The great American myth is that they want to accept us, to shower us with their precious American equality and democracy. Yes, sir (not *sí, señor*), provided we transform ourselves in their image, forgetting Spanish and surrendering to their way of life.

What an illusion. When will it dawn on us that they never will accept us as equals? And it's not just about skin color. It's really about *burro* work. If they were to accept us as equals in their universities, in their professions, if they truly educated our children in their public institutions, who would do the work of *burros*? Who would harvest the fields, who would dig in the mines, who would labor for endless hours in the *maquiladoras*, who would slave away in the canneries, who would pave the streets, who would wash the dirty dishes, who would clean the rest rooms, the toilets, the johns, the shit holes? Who?...

...with what dexterity you assuaged my fears, removing one by one the cumbersome veils that covered my body.

Oh, you destitute souls! How can you survive in that mud shack? Where do you play? What do you eat for breakfast? Do you know where this train comes from, and where it's headed, or does your world end where the white desert sinks into the horizon?

When I jotted down random thoughts in my notebook, I never intended for them to end up in a manuscript. At first I took notes because it seemed appropriate, the thing to do at the beginning of a trip. Many years later, on the kind of lazy afternoon that could inspire one to poke around in the ashes of the past, I found the notorious little notebook. Upon perusing it, I felt happy to have recovered a piece of my past, something that I had allowed to slip away and gather dust in the obscure attic of my brain. I also felt slightly amused to discover that there was a time in my life when I had been so ingenuous. The notes regarding the actual traveling, that is, moving through space on a train from the Border to Mexico City, opened the floodgates of memory.

I was visited by voices and images that I had repressed long ago. During several days I just sat and remembered. What really surprised me was that the memory of him had not been even slightly altered by the years, by maturity, by experience, or by whatever it was that mediated between the present and a past which until that afternoon had been locked up in a chest and forgotten. Memory came wrapped in passionate hues and romantic flourishes, and I say memory because after arriving in Mexico City, I had abandoned my good intention to document my adventures in that little notebook. There was not one single entry about him. So I had no notes to read, only memories that came back to me in a rush. And one letter.

I can't say exactly when I decided to gather the entries from the journal and the post-journey memories, and put them all together in a manuscript. I guess I should blame the entries. Although they were ingenuous, as I said before, it seemed to me they revealed a certain reflective attitude that might interest persons who at that

time were so engaged in uncovering female voices (not to
mention Chicana voices) that until a very short while ago
had remained hidden behind canonized Western icons.
(Not the least bit modest, you will say. The truth is that
modesty disappears slowly with the years and with the
travesties that life delivers unto us.)

Once I decided to put it all together in some sort of
text, it seemed logical to begin at the beginning and to
proceed in chronological order until arriving at the end,
although I must admit that I was not the least bit certain
what end would be reached. As you've probably noticed
that's not the way things turned out. As I proceeded to type
(to edit, to shape, to invent?) the entries that somehow
seemed more authentic and objective precisely because
they were actual notes, I was flooded by non-recorded
memories, certainly less empirical but in no way less
insistent. Almost imperceptibly I began to mix notes and
recalled events (*and what about the fantasies?*). It seems
a bit overwrought to mention the fact that the whole thing
turned into a carnival, a veritable hodgepodge of past
and present and future. Initially I had planned to divide
the story into two parts: 1) the journey, and 2) being
there. (The return trip didn't interest me in the least,
particularly because I had flown back in a marijuana-
induced stupor, and scarcely remembered the flight.)
For several days the loss of chronological order bothered
me, but in the end I conceded that what was supposed
to be Part Two was also part of the journey, if not in the
geo-spatial sense, certainly in a spiritual sense. Thus,
it didn't need its own, separate part. But then you've
probably already figured that one out.

Sorry, love, for being late. Did I tell you we were going to meet with Dolores Huerta, who is in the city to meet with local unions? Well, Beto made the arrangements. You knew he had worked with Chávez when he first began to organize in California, didn't you? Beto wanted us to meet her, so we agreed to get together at Sanborns at 11:00. She had a meeting at Los Pinos at 9:00 and of course, they were caught in a traffic jam when they left and we had to wait for her until 12:30. But believe me, it was worth it. She is truly an extraordinary person. She spoke to us so patiently about her activities with the Union and about her dreams for the farm workers. And she was actually interested in us; she wanted to know why we're here, how things are going for us, and she invited us to work with the UFW when we return to the States. Well, maybe I will someday. I don't know, Sergio. For the moment I prefer not to think about that, but someday I guess I'll have to go back, won't I?

I have to admit that I was really impressed by her. She's a simple yet truly dynamic person, but what's more important, she's so straightforward. She has about a dozen kids, but that doesn't keep her from being one of the most active leaders in the Union. We were all fascinated. We wanted her to drop by Casa Aztlán to eat with us but you can imagine her itinerary. After she left, the rest of us just couldn't separate. We felt as if we'd been with a prophet. We felt spiritually uplifted and we wanted to talk a while, to prolong our collective sense of inspiration. Well, the conversation ended as usual with a long and animated speech by Beto. You know how he loves to treat us as if we were his disciples. Well, in a sense we are. It's through his eyes that we are forced to analyze and order everything that we read and everything that we study at the UNAM and in the reading circles, linking it all to our reality, attempting to reach some sort of understanding of the historical processes that forged the Chicano experience (forgive me for resorting to a cliché, but that's how Beto puts it).

Believe it or not, we're getting along much better. I have learned to respect him a lot, and I appreciate the dedication and affection with which he guides us (although the affectionate part is something we have to guess at, since it's hard for him to show it). Even Isaura, whom he sometimes drives totally bonkers with his macho charade, secretly respects him, even though she'd never admit it. I guess that little by little he's letting go of his patriarchal attitude and learning as much from the women as we are from him, because believe me, we don't for a single moment lighten up on our plan to sensitize him. I think he's finally realizing how absurd it is to talk about oppression if that talk doesn't include a space for women's issues. There are women in your organization, right? And they're equal participants, aren't they? It just takes so long to break through the layers and layers of cultural brainwashing. But it's possible, wouldn't you say? Very difficult, but possible.

Well anyway, after saying goodbye, I got on the bus and as I rode along, I was trying to give shape, or maybe even a name, to the experiences I've had since arriving in Mexico. As you know, I came here for purely egotistical reasons. I wanted to recover a personal past; although my quest was somewhat spiritual, I also wanted to have a great time. I had finished my degree, and it was time to face the real world, be responsible, find a job and all, but I felt a need to go through some sort of ritual. Moreover, since I enrolled at the university where there were very few of us, and those that did grace the hallowed halls of academia tended to suffer a deracinating metamorphosis (as Beto would say), I felt that with each new social interaction an essential part of me was reduced even further. What I'm trying to say is that the waters of assimilation were dragging me downstream like Rulfo's poor Serpentina. There were rumors floating around —about Chávez and Tijerina— but our families warned

Chic. Neurosis

140   Erlinda Gonzales-Berry

us that those rabble-rousers had nothing to do with our lives. Fortunately, it was not possible to totally escape their influence. And who would have guessed, here I am in Mexico, discovering the Chicano Movement. But there are times when I feel as if everything is a bit artificial here, and I really ought to return in order to take advantage of a more practical education. I have to get back there in order to experience in flesh and blood this extraordinary phenomenon.

I was thinking too that we Chicanos (that sounds good, *we Chicanos*) represent some sort of hybridity or syncretism. Over there we are so acutely aware of our marginal position, our defensive stance in relation to a foreign and chaotic space, that we are in a state of constant tension vis à vis that otherness that confronts us every day. We feel permanently threatened; with every step we expect someone to trip us, either literally or figuratively. I have baptized this constant state of alertness "Chicano Neurosis" —a neurosis, or a double consciousness, that afflicts all marginalized human beings— and please note that I don't use this term in a negative sense because it is precisely this neurosis, our exalted state of self-consciousness, that compels us to assert ourselves and go beyond the obstacles set up by a society that openly rejects us. Faced with that threatening alterity, we offer our myth of Mexicanness as an opposing force. We insist on our Mexican fiestas, our music, our *quinceañeras*, and on symbols like the Virgin of Guadalupe, which you have told me are losing their significance in modern Mexico; and now with the Chicano Movement, we conjure up new symbols, some of them recuperated from the ashes of moments that perhaps have lost their vitality for your compatriots.

I know, for example, that you all find it hilarious that we reclaim Pre-Columbian myths with which we nurture our emerging ideology. Nonetheless, you yourselves conjured up these myths in a not-too-distant past, and you can't deny it because you'd be denying Rivera and Orozco, Paz and Fuentes. But all of that cultural artifice, regardless of how anachronistic it may appear to you, is a necessary stage in our path to self-determination. We must nurture ourselves on something, and those myths and symbols make us strong because they permit us to rescue our history from oblivion. Furthermore, they are our amulets against that demon that rejects us even as it seeks to devour us. But then we come here, and suddenly it becomes obvious that we are not Mexicans. We feel disoriented because our alterity here —perhaps less hostile— turns out to be precisely what functions as our haven over there. And here's the real irony: there are moments when I feel inclined to offer my "Angloness" as a reaction to the alienation that plagues me in your space.

But listen, I think that after suffering so many trials and psychological tribulations —and of course I am aware of the fact that everything is relative and on the seismic scale of human convulsions, my afflictions are only silent farts— in the end we are neither Anglos nor Mexicans. We occupy a unique space somewhere between these two poles. Our space is characterized on the surface by shades of both elements of the dichotomy. Nonetheless, in its deep structure, there lies something new. I believe there will come a time when we no longer feel obliged to offer our Mexicanness, but rather our Chicanoness, in response to our circumstances. A time when we will be free to affirm our Chicano neurosis, just as Leopoldo Zea exhorts Latin Americans to affirm their barbarity and to use it as a theoretical framework to define the Western world, that foreign reality that sought to disparage all things American, to view them as barbarian. It seems to me that Chicanismo and barbarism are analogous notions; in both cases a negative is turned into a positive and becomes a motive for self-definition and self-determination.

You are absolutely right, my love, the danger lies in getting stuck forever in the false security of cultural essentialism or in cultural solutions to a universal problem, because that would separate us from the marginalized peoples of the world. I understand very clearly that the analysis I have just expounded upon

has its limits; however, I believe it's a necessary step on
the path toward liberation. An oppressed community
(How empty that expression sounds... What shall we do
to restore its significance?)...   Anyway, an oppressed
community has to know who it is and assimilate its
history if it is to know itself as part of all oppressed
communities.

And yes, I do realize that there is an enormous gap
between word and action. You, for example, are a model
of someone who has reconciled those two aspects of
commitment. But it is so much harder on the other side,
do you understand? Perhaps because we live amidst
such opulence, and because our system has so cleverly
manipulated racism so as to avoid the coming together
and the collaboration of the various marginalized groups,
talk is cheap and action minimal. At this very moment,
what is happening over there is out of the ordinary and
I don't doubt for one moment that within a few years
all but our memories of the Movement will have been
co-opted.

And now, to shift gears just a bit, because I see your
beautiful eyes drooping, you, my dear Sergio, think I
haven't the slightest inkling of what is going on, but I do
know that you went to Guerrero this weekend and I also
know that something went wrong, because I can see that
you are depressed and each day your eyes appear more
melancholy. Oh, Sergio, embrace me, hold me close. You
don't know how much I worry about you. Please love me,
Sergio, love me.

You have probably asked yourselves more than once why it is that I have given him neither voice nor body. I can't say that I fully understand my own motives. Nonetheless, I offer you a few possibilities that crop into my mind as my fingers scamper across the keyboard: 1) I saw this technique in the novel of a Mexican writer and I was very impressed by it; 2) I don't remember him very well, or I remember him too well and the pain of that memory is so sweet that I have no desire to share it; 3) he really is the reader with whom Mari desires to enter into an intimate relationship; and 4) there will be those of you who say that he never existed, since he is nothing more than the projection of her/my/our particular vision of the ideal male; in other words: the Second Sex inventing the First, the way we would like him to be.

...My mistake was to confuse pleasure with love, is that not so? I cared so much for you; I offered the most precious gift I had to give, and you refused to accept it... Listen to me, Mari, what you propose is absurd. I've never considered matrimony an option. I like my life just as it is, and feel no need to change it. Besides, you're too young. If you tied yourself down with the responsibilities of marriage, and worse yet, of having a child, you'd be squandering your youth. If you wish, we can keep seeing each other as we have been, with no strings attached. I would like that very much. But if you can't accept these conditions, do whatever it is you have to do. Some day you'll understand that what I'm doing is for your own good.

So who are you to tell me what's good for me? What's going on here is that you are too self-centered to accept responsibility. All you're interested in is having a good time without commitment and I think that sucks. Anyway, isn't it time to break in a new virgin? I know your little tricks and I bet what you're really afraid of is missing out on one of your great pleasures, initiating neophytes.

Mari, don't say such foolish things. I know this is very painful but believe me, marriage would be a disaster for both of us...

How wonderful, Sergio, to be back here with you again. Well, to be honest the beach was divine, but the so-called human beings who hang out there leave much to be desired. First of all, when we arrived, totally terrified after our first long trip by bus, we couldn't find a taxi to take us to the hotel. Finally, a young dude, about twenty or so, approached us and said he'd give us a lift. We asked him if he was a taxi driver, since we noticed he didn't have one of those lights on the roof of his car and he said yes, his company was on strike but he was working *clandestinamente* –that's how he put it– because he had to make a living. You tell me, what could we do? There we were, all revved up in high party-gear, and stranded at the bus station.

So we haggled a bit with him and finally agreed on a price. As we got in the car I noticed there was another dude who was driving, a gigolo type with his leather jacket, hair dyed not exactly blond but something more along the color of tangerines, and well-toasted skin. That's right, one of those beach-boy types. The four of us got in the back seat, Toña, Lupe, Julie and I, and the other guy sat up front. Right off the bat, I began to feel uncomfortable about the whole thing, my typical fears –as my friends have labelled them– but I didn't say anything. And the gigolo kept staring at Julie in the rear view mirror. There we were, all set to go, but he didn't start the car; we just sat there for a while, until I finally asked what was wrong. One of our union bosses is parked over there and we don't want him to see us, said the gigolo as he stared intensely at Julie's image in the mirror. After a long pause, he started up the car but we didn't move an inch. Then I saw the gigolo flash his lights, off-on-off-on, you know, as if he were signaling to someone.

Suddenly, in lurid Technicolor, a scene from Macon County Line flashed before my eyes. Don't tell me those movies haven't made it down here? Believe me, it's no loss. You're better off never having seen that shit. What I saw was a deserted beach, I mean not even one single sea gull, then three carloads of hoodlums surrounding the "taxi" and the orange-haired gigolo, still undressing Julie with his eyes, pulls out an enormous machete while he spits through his teeth, they're yours, fellas, all except the blond one; she's mine. And that was the whole scene, but that's all it took for my blood pressure to shoot up. I started to sweat like a stuck pig. When I could no longer stand it, I announced, excuse me I think I'm going to throw up, I need some fresh air. As polite as a first-class gentleman, the second dude opened the door and helped me get out. I dashed toward a policeman that was strolling down the street. He looked at me in disbelief as I prattled, please listen, those guys offered to take us to our hotel but we don't know if they're really taxi drivers because they're acting rather strangely. I think they're contemplating taking us hostage, then raping us. What do you suggest we do? MeanwhileToña, seeing me head toward the policeman, became frightened and took out her knife —supposedly she uses it to peel fruits and carries it with her everywhere— just in case. Then finally the cop recovered from his what-the-hell-got-into-this-chick trance and he waved to a taxi that had just parked in front of the bus station. Hey Chemo, take these Pochas to their hotel, and you young ladies, *háganme el favor,* don't accept rides from strangers (as if Chemito were our life-long friend).

So, off we went, packed like sardines in a Volkswagen driven by a taxi driver who was friendlier than a used-car salesman. When we finally arrived at the Hotel Faro, Lupe asked me what had happened at the station. When I told them about my premonition, they just about died laughing and they began to taunt me, Oh Mari, you're so melodramatic! You're not a kid anymore. How are we going to have a good time if you're always so *friquiada?* (That's Chicano for freaked out, in case you didn't know.) What a bunch of ingrates, is what I say. I had just saved their lives, and they were anything but grateful. If you're not grateful, you're hateful, as my mamá would say. They left me no choice but to say, fine, from now on I won't say a word; I will just follow your lead and see what happens. Right on, Mari, way to own up. Well, hold on to your britches, dear boy, and I will tell you in colorful detail how those sweet, wanna-be-liberated friends of mine got us into a fine fix.

Wait, get comfy. Hand me that pillow. Put your legs over here. You want a smoke? Lend me your lighter. Not that one, you clown. Okay, baby. STORY TIME.

After resting for a bit, we went to the beach, where we were blissfully absorbing our vitamin D when some Germans approached us. We started flirting with them, asking them where they were from, what they were doing in Mexico and so on. Of course we didn't tell them we were from the other side; we said we were from Mexico City. After the sun had set they invited us for a drink and then to dinner, but first they had to stop by their hotel for some money.

When we arrived at the hotel I plopped myself in an easy chair in the lobby. It was hotter than hell outside. Then the one named Hans began bugging us, please come to our room, darlinks. They had good tequila he promised, and Noche Buena. Well upon hearing the magic label, I jumped from my seat and we all headed toward the elevator. They poured drinks and we sat around chatting. No problems, we could understand them perfectly well. Lots of apicoalveolar s's, a castillian zeta, a lateral palatal *elle* (double l). Like this, listen up: [eṣpaŋa], [ɵapato], [kaʎe]. In short, very Madridian their Spanish. Of course, we were impressed because they had a suite with two bedrooms, two baths, a kitchen and living room, all very neatly arranged. I don't have to repeat that they were Germans.

I was working on my second glass of tequila when Hans went to the bedroom and returned with a bag. He opened it and pulled out a video camera and a small television. When he was done assembling everything, I noticed that we were all appearing on the TV screen. Lupe was ecstatic —you know what a ham she is, being a dancer and all. Now Toña, who's a bit timid, kept trying to hide and Julie stayed cool as a cucumber, as always. No, Sergio, I don't think it's a sexual allusion, just an idiomatic –or idiotic– expression, meaning laid back or easy-going. Well everyone began to take turns at the camera except me, of course. I don't know why, but I began to feel a bit uncomfortable and said to Julie: I smell a rat. Lupe heard me and was quick to interject, Oh, Mari, quit being so uptight. Just then one of the guys, I think his name was Peter, said, don't you think it's too hot in here? and there goes his t-shirt, leaving him in his swimsuit, and I don't mean trunks, I mean an itsy bitsy bikini. What can I say, they're shameless. I've always heard that they're the first ones to get buck naked at the Costa del Sol. Right away Lupe, who must have a German ancestor somewhere in her family tree, followed his example and took off the t-shirt and skirt she had thrown on over her bathing suit.

Then Hans took the camera and began to focus on Lupe, all the while calling out *kommt mal, zieht euch aus, kleine Häschen* which according to Peter means come on little rabbits, take off your clothes. I was disgusted by the whole thing. Call it intuition or simply common sense, but just as I announced I was going back to the hotel, Erik walks out of the other bedroom with a P39 Walther. Steve had one. Haven't I told you about Steve? I thought I had. Nevermind, that's another story, one of these afternoons I'll fill you in. Then Erik said, hey guys, look what I bought at the *mercado* this afternoon. At the *mercado*, can you believe that? What do you think of it? And he looked at me as he said it. I got the message, babe. I quickly pulled off my t-shirt and sat down, pretending that I was a willing player in this cat-and-mouse game that was about to become somewhat grotesque. My friends? Totally out of it; it was as if they were hypnotized. They didn't get the picture. They just kept dancing around like free spirits and that evil little camera eye kept following them around. I just watched, completely horrified, waiting for a scandalous scene to unfold and Erik kept playing with his Walther, caressing it and glancing repeatedly in my direction.

Suddenly I got an idea. I jumped from my chair and threw off my skirt. Of course I had my bathing suit on, the bikini you like so much. I ran and wrapped my arms around Hans and began to kiss his ear. And believe me, he was quick to respond. Let's go to the bedroom. Okay, I replied. Shall we take the camera? Hold your horses, I said, I like a warm-up first. He laughed as he led the way. No one noticed that we had left. Upon entering the bedroom, I quickly glanced around. When I bent over to take off my sandals, the brute grasped my right arm, twisted it behind my back and threw me on the bed. Hans, Hans, if you want to be a tiger, first you must be a kitten. Slow down, I said. Look, you just lie there and let me open the door to pleasures not even imagined in northern climates. We Mexicans know the erotic secrets of the Aztecs, passed on to the chosen by Coyolxauhqui. Secrets practiced only by trained virgins on warrior prisoners, on the eve of their sacrifice. Hans opened his eyes wide and said, Oh darlink, I am your prisoner!

I took two shirts from the closet, tore them into strips with which I tied him to the bed and gagged his mouth, but not before having removed the sheets. From the other room I heard someone yell in a rather threatening voice, "I told you to take it off." That's what gave me the courage to do what I knew I had to do. Quickly I knotted the sheets together and tied one end to the bed frame. I opened the window; I got nauseated looking down eight floors, but I didn't let that keep me from letting myself go. I never asked myself where I expected to end up. Fortunately the sheet almost reached the balcony below us. When I heard the delicate squeals of well-bred women, I knew there were people on the balcony. Two men grabbed my dangling legs and helped me land on the balcony. Dear girl, said one of the men, there are better ways to commit suicide. Listen please, I need help. I explained as fast as I could that my friends were in danger.

Later, I learned that the gentleman who called at the German's door and announced with a voice of authority that Señorita Lupe Quiñones had an emergency call in the lobby, was a Peruvian General on vacation in Acapulco. That night he and his wife took us all out to dinner. Oh yes, the young ladies. Well they marched out in a row as if nothing had happened, pulling on their t-shirts, bidding farewell to the Germans, bye fellows, ciao ciao, thanks for everything. The Germans stood at the door with their mouths open and their eyes on fire. When the General got off at the seventh floor we began to howl with laughter and kept it up as we made our way through the lobby and down the street until we reached the Faro. And now and then my charming friends would exclaim, Oh Mari, silly, melodramatic Mari, you snatched us from the claws of the devil.

Well, my guess is that sooner or later they found him tied to the bed, don't you think?

Afterwards we had some experiences that were less harrowing. As I said, we went to dinner with the general and then, abandoning our original plan to look for dates, decided to revel in our feminine company. What can I say, our first trip to Sin City, Mexico had its good moments. But you know something Sergio, I missed you so much. In fact, we talked a lot about you. My friends just can't believe that I can come and go as I please, even date other guys if I like, that I tell you everything, and we still keep caring deeply and passionately about each other. They can't believe that you don't get jealous or act as if I were your private property. I keep having to remind them that Sergio is not your average guy. He's the rare bird who truly believes in liberty and who lives his ideology. I'm not kidding, Sergio; you are very special.

And now, darlink, I am your prisoner, so realize upon my body your most secret desires.

Señorita. This is Aguascalientes. You can get off for a while if you like, but don't wander too far away. We don't want to leave you behind, blondie. Please don't call me blondie. Don't you see that I'm not a Gringa? Can't you see that I'm like you, darker than a moonless night? Pochita, then. Can I call you Pochita?

...Jackass, call me whatever you please because I can just imagine what you're thinking. Great tits, what an ass. Yes, that's exactly what you're thinking, brother, it's written all over your face. Do you really think I enjoy your undressing me with your eyes while you instinctively grab your balls? The truth is that my friend got it right. She made up an imaginary dialog when she was traveling through Mexico by bus. Is everything under control, sir? Was that a negative on your self-exam for cancer of the testicles? Do you really think I like it? Jeez, you are such an imbecile. How little you know about females. What myths you Latin Lobers have invented to keep your women under your thumb! The eleventh commandment of the sacred and masculine Mediterranean Catholic Church (and curiously the only one that is stated in the affirmative): 11) Objectify them; thus will you assure yourself the kingdom of earth, for objects are helpless against masculine power and prerogative...

It's true Sergio, I promised to tell you about Steve. But now that whole story seems so far away and frivolous that there's nothing special about it. You're right, it's part of my past, and as such, it would be absurd to deny it. Let's see, I would have to begin with what I remember the most —oh, yeah, the pain.

There was a time when I felt so offended and wounded that I thought I would never recover. Now I see that was the reaction of a weak and immature ego. After all, I was young, and my experience with boyfriends had been extremely limited, because my parents were always very strict. And as far as sex is concerned, forget it. My deep fear of confession had left me no choice but virginity. But with Steve everything happened in the most natural way. He was older than I, which in itself was out of the ordinary, because over there young folks tend to mix only with people their own age. At first it was a beautiful adventure, but as our relationship developed something strange began to happen. I began to feel overwhelmed by something —how can I say it— something almost instinctual that made me want to have a child with him —a daughter, a son, it didn't matter which— and I began to insist on marriage. Now that I think about it I see that it was a trick of my subconscious mind, a smoke screen raised to hide the true motive, or perhaps I should say the true motives, because nothing is so clear cut that it can be attributed to a single motive, right?

Generally it's men who objectify women in order to dominate them, but in this case, I was the one who began to feel, as the writer we call Elena would have said, *an insistent and implacable need to ascribe it all to the love that comes in the dark,* and then to confuse love with the right to ownership. I forced myself to believe that marriage, a simple structural framework imposed by legal decrees and social customs for economic reasons, would

grant me the exclusive right to own him. Although I'm
not sure I can clarify the motives behind my attitude, we
could speculate that it all had to do with my immaturity
and with the fact that this was my first affair. Add to
that the fact that since infancy, practically since sucking
at my mother's breast, I was nourished with inspiring
fairy tales and held them always as paradigms for my
adult behavior. As a child, night after night I begged
my mother, my sweet, sweet *mami*, to open the door
to dream land with the lovely images of Cinderella, and
over and over again she gave in, believing that she was
doing me a great favor, as she recited word for word, like
melodious notes on a clavichord, my favorite fairy tale.
Can't you see that since childhood I dreamed of the day
that my gorgeous Prince Charming would arrive, place
my delicate foot in the glass slipper, and sweep me away
to live in his castle in the clouds? In this case we'd have
to replace the glass slipper with a rubber diaphragm but,
at any rate, my prince charming materialized. Since we
didn't go immediately to live in our castle in the clouds,
I soon began to feel guilty for having become involved
in an illicit affair. (How absurd, isn't it, to reduce a
relationship between two people who care for each other
to such language).

Sometimes all I could think about was what would
happen if he left me. What would become of me? I
was possessed by an incredible fear that was a result of
the following, inbred reasoning: now that I had tasted
the forbidden fruits, and I had rather learned to enjoy
them, what would I do to avoid giving in to sins of the
flesh with other men if he left me? After dwelling ad
nauseam on this absurd notion, I decided that my only
salvation lay in the sacred state of marriage, which would
grant me respectability and at the same time save me
from becoming a citizen of *putalandia*. He, of course,
refused to concede, so we broke up. According to him,
he wouldn't be helping me any by marrying me; what's
more, some day I would wake up and appreciate the
favor he was doing me (well, he was sure doing me, but I
wouldn't call that a favor). Naturally, I was destroyed. Oh

Sergio, you're so cute; so you think I ruined it all because of my imperialist attitude, and my Catholic neurosis. Only you would think of seeing it that way, but in the end, maybe you're right.

That happened shortly before I came to Mexico. On the train down here, I wrote him a very bitter letter blaming him for everything. I guess it was my way of getting even. But nevertheless, in these last months that I've been with you, I think I've learned an important lesson: you can't posses another human being. Although it's natural to want to spend every moment of the day with the one you love, it's really important for both parties to keep some measure of independence. If you don't do that, you fail as a couple. Oh, come on, spare me. I'm way past believing in sins of the flesh, or of any other kind. I think I've finally unloaded my cultural baggage and my gender-bound socialization. This body is mine and I shall be the one who decides what to do with it. Whenever I want to have a daughter, I will do so because that's what I truly want to do and not because I want to trap a man. And, believe me, it's not that I believe in gratuitous and irresponsible intimacy, but rather that I have simply demystified those social decrees designed to keep women at home, barefoot and pregnant, and their men working like mules to support them. The incredible thing about all of this is that I have survived, and I've somehow escaped being drowned in a whirlpool of pathological complexes. I wonder why it is, Sergio, that the most natural thing in life becomes so complicated. Oh, you believe we're being manipulated by capitalist propaganda? I think you're absolutely right. One just has to watch the ads to see that. It truly is a miracle that there are not more sexually impaired people inhabiting this world.

Okay, now it's your turn to relate some personal rite of passage. You could give it a title, *From Adolescence to Maturity: The Adventures of a Young Latin Lober*. I know, you're a man of few words and you'd rather shoot your wad than shoot the breeze. Well, I offer myself without an ounce of resistance, and let's see, darlink, what secrets you have in store for me today.

*Let us do something we have never done before,
says the young and innocent Mariel Hemingway to
Woody Allen.*

Paleeeetaas. We've got strawberry, we've got banana, we've got lemon, tamarind and guava popsicles. Come and get your *paleeetaaas.*

...Should I buy one, for old times' sake? A tamarind or a guava *paleta,* I can almost taste it already. Whatever you do, don't drink the water and don't eat those street popsicles. They're made from sewer water and they'll give you such a case of Montezuma's revenge, you'll just shit yourself to death. What a bunch of bull, Montezuma's revenge. It's an initiation rite: a scatological initiation to the Third World. Return your system to its natural ecological state. Restore all the precious germs to that clean, whitewashed, sterilized system of yours. Why postpone the inevitable? But not on the train. I'd better wait until I get to Mexico City. Then I'll buy at least ten popsicles, two each of my favorite flavors, and initiate myself in grand style. Have no fear, Pepto Bismol is here. Wow, what a foot-in-the-mouth blunder one of our ex-chiefs of national government committed the time he came to Mexico and announced, right there in front of the TV cameras that he loved Mexico, despite the fact that Montezuma tried to get even with Uncle Sam by punishing him. He actually said that he was glad to be able to take up jogging again, back and forth to the bathroom. I love that commercial where this guy, a Latin Lober type, appears in front of a New York hotel and rattles off —in Spanish no less— on gringolandia TV: I took a trip to New York and got such an incredible case of diarrhea. *Gracias a Dios* I brought my Pepto. Two points for writer of commercial number 390,568. So, what should I do? To shit or not to shit. On the train, I mean, that is the question. *Chale,* I better wait.

So you mean to tell me that you spent the entire rest stop in Aguascalientes thinking about excrement and

Pepto Bismol? I can't believe it. You're sick....

Come on, blondie, I mean Pochita, we're leaving now. What did you think of Aguastibias?

...Oh my, how you've changed. Now you use such a familiar tone. And you're making jokes, changing the name of the town from Aguascalientes (Hot Water) to Aguastibias (Tepid Water). We still have one night of travel left and you're thinking about how tonight things could go the other way, from tepid to hot, and you might get to play Latin Lober in my berth. Right, flat face (that one's for you, Denise Chávez), damn fool *Machón Mexicón* (I think that's more or less how José Agustín said it). I would say that went from tepid to cold, wouldn't you?

Jesus, I don't know why I get so worked up; I'm always on guard, ready to fight anyone who looks at me sideways. These poor guys, what else can you expect? They're products of their environment; if they're machos it's because their circumstances force them to be. I don't know why I get so uptight when they're so brazen about displaying their carnal appetites. Actually, there's no great difference between Latinos and white boys. They all aspire to the same thing but the ones over there are more subtle. That whole thing about how you interest me as a person, I really care about how you feel, what you think, your world vision, all that's pure bullshit. In the end their goals are exactly the same, only their methods are different. After all is said and done, what they're really interested in finding is a moist space in which to rest (what do you mean "rest", don't you think you ought to write "thrust"?) their infamous and precarious masculinity. Come on now, don't act so delicate; forget the euphemisms; name the sacred instrument, vehicle and carrier of the masculine ego, the word made flesh, obscene extension, cause of our dread, object of our desire, the male thing, the dick, the pecker, the hose, the tool, the wanker, the wand, the Johnson, the monk, Saint Peter, the general, the pistol, the lollipop, the diplomat, the dip-stick, the lizard, the ding-dong, the bush-beater, the serpent, the hero, the lullaby, the cock, the whip, the flute, the know-it-all, the schlonge, the pump, the hambone, the dart of Venus, the magic wand, the sausage, the Pee-Wee. Now then, don't you feel better after having called it by its names? Isn't it true that naming things is one way of taking that first breath of freedom?

Oh, the games you —you?, I mean, we women— play: that's a word I mustn't say, I don't do those things, you can touch me but just for a moment, only here and not there, because I'm saving myself for my future husband and besides, I don't want you to think I'm a whore. What you all, I mean we all, need to do is ask ourselves if we like it or we don't like it. And if the answer is affirmative, we should admit it, proclaim it, and for God's sake, put an end to the games. Because if we don't, our bodies and our lives will be controlled forever by our husbands, priests, and yes, by our mothers, too, in spite of themselves. That's right, admit it and shout at the top of our voices: I LIKE IT AND I DO IT JUST BECAUSE I LIKE IT and not because it's my conjugal obligation, or because you want a son, or because I'm a whore. Very simply say: I do it because it pleases me, and I damn-well feel like doing it. A priest should have nothing to say about it. I arrived at that conclusion a while ago and I quit confessing because I could no longer stand that insipid and repressive ritual: Bless me father for I have sinned...I petted three times. Above or below the waist? Once above and twice below. Over or under your clothes? Once over his clothes, once over and once under mine. And what good did quitting confession do? It's not like I ran out the next day and offered my little jewel to the first male I encountered. So deeply rooted is the repression that eats away at us and denies us our humanity that it's not a simple matter of sloughing it off as if it were nothing. I wonder what it's like to be a güera? To be free of all those complexes inculcated by our religion and by our patriarchal culture. That suspicion I have of white women is nothing more than a cover for my fear: fear of my flesh, fear of my femaleness, fear of my very essence. Shit, where are those damn cigarettes?

You know something? I don't understand you; first

you complain about men and white chicks for being so aggressive, then you flaunt a no-holds-barred sexuality for all women. Well, look, that bit about white women is nothing more than petty envy. Don't you understand that our whole lives we've been told that beauty comes only in tall, blond packages? And why deny it, we too are victims of vanity and brainwashing that has convinced us that we're sex objects, so we're out of luck because you know that bit about how climatic conditions in southern hemispheres only yield short and dark products. Well, the blond part we can take care of with a bottle of peroxide, right? But, tell me, how are we going to get any taller? Sorry, honey, the only remedy to this dilemma is to accept our condition and spend the rest of our lives feeling super-inferior because we're not *la rubia que todos quieren*. Everybody loves a blond (or a light beer), as the commercial declares. And to really top it off, besides beauty they've got the liberty and freedom that their culture provides. So if I complain about white chicks, there you have it; my attitude is nothing more than a deep resentment nourished by an insidious psychological manipulation that immobilizes us and denies us the right to develop our full human potential.

And so far as men are concerned, I just get so damn mad when they abuse women. But I think their attitude becomes abusive, and please note that I'm talking only about the sexual realm, not of the thousands of other facets of women's' oppression by men —although maybe in the long run they're the same thing— precisely because women have not, *we* have not, accepted our sexuality. We repress it and we invent all these petty games, waiting for men, denying our desires, always playing the role of victim. That way we absolve ourselves of doing what we have been made to believe is sinful, because how can the victim be guilty? (And you well know that the axis, the fundamental principle upon which our culture is based and from which it nourishes itself is guilt). Meanwhile, the male is forced to be the aggressor, to sing at our balcony, to stalk his victim, and hence the development of all the subtle and not-so-subtle repressive aspects of what should be an intimate and liberating human act, but that somehow has been distorted and dehumanized by social rules designed to keep everyone in place: there we have the young boys, inventing and creating the world; over here, the little girls, cultivating the optimum conditions for gestation and for the encouragement of male creativity and genius.

Whoa, girl, aren't you giving yourself a major headache with all that deep thinking?...

Once again it was a turbulent event that took us to the very edge of the abyss where an atavistic and primordial undercurrent annihilated all traces of a separate consciousness, with our gender stigmas, the positive and negative signs inexorably magnetized, deposited in the oneiric waters of a cosmic lake where we swam effortlessly in a thick uterine substance. I pictured myself in other times, in other places, swimming in these same waters, first in a stairwell at a pub, one of those that smell of raw wood and constitute the vital center of every European village, with a crude man, a drunk farmer who begged me to leave my barmaid job and go live with him in his stone hut, built with the very hands that clumsily fondled me; then in a tepee in one of those vast plains where the howling wind almost drowns out the maddening voices of coyotes, with a young warrior who had not yet washed off the war paint but whose tender caresses belied the ferocity with which he had moments before slashed ten scalps off the skulls of pale-eyed men.

I tried to tell you about these other lives that emerged from my subconscious which I was sure of having experienced before, but you, being the stubborn cynic that you are in all that has to do with the spiritual realm and especially regarding reincarnation, smiled tenderly and between long inhalations of smoke, asked me how I could continue believing in that foolishness after your having explained to me countless times the dialectical and material base of human existence.

— I had to admit that I didn't know, because truly I believe you and I've devoured all you've given me to read and I've absorbed it all, but suddenly I get these images and feelings that are so *cómo se dice,* so powerful, so intense, and so entangled in my subconscious that I can't just deny them. They come from the same place as the dream I always had when I was a child and had a fever, and in that dream I appeared with my aunts, all of them dressed in navy blue dresses with white polka dots, kneeling before Roman soldiers on horseback who delivered whiplashes to our backs; where could that dream come from if I knew nothing of Rome or of Romans, I was still illiterate and it was a time before there was any television; I had no knowledge of the world and its history. Where do you think it came from? It's always been a mystery, but it comes from the same place as these images because they can't be memories, they're more like intuitions, perhaps they are memories of the flesh but not of the mind, when I make love...

Oh, darling, quit being so histrionic, grab onto objective analysis because if you don't you'll never climb out of that cesspool of subjectivity that blinds you to material reality.

I know, I know, but you don't understand that I have no control over this aspect of my being; perhaps they issue forth from the right hemisphere of my brain... what do you think?

You're quick to reply, oh dear, there you go on another tangent; don't you see that it's all the same crap, inventions of cretins designed to keep the human race in a state of perpetual ignorance in order to better fill the globe with churches and more and more things, with objects, with knickknacks that we don't need but without which we couldn't live because every time we turn around they push them in our face, they shove them in our brain and even up our asses in order to keep alive a dehumanizing anachronistic system that places more value on an object than on a human being?

I know, I know, I said, let's just change the subject because I know that my ignorance exasperates you, but believe me, my love, I want to learn from you, I want you to fill me with you, your body, your ideas and everything that you are, but right now I want to talk about something else, I want to talk about love; do you believe that love is possible?

And you, cautiously trying to avoid a trap, say well, I

don't know if what you and I have is love but I like you, I care for you very very much, I want to be with you, I don't ever tire of making love with you.

And I, treading once again *that dangerous territory of confusing love with eternity* (ay, Elena, you sure got that right) but do you believe that this can last all our lives, like the love between my parents, my grandparents' love; that reminds me, I have some letters that my grandpa wrote my grandma before they were married. They were first cousins (but not really, not by blood anyway, because my grandfather was adopted) and they lived in the country; the two families lived together so it was very easy for them to fall in love. She was thirteen and he eighteen when they began to write; the family had several ranches and they sent him to work at different ones, so he would write to her and send his letters with anyone who happened by and, listen, he said things like this:

Créeme que cada día te quiero más y para el 25 de julio solo con la muerte te faltaré. Deveras te quiero de todo corazón aun si no fuera pecado más que a mi Dios. Si tú me amaras tanto como yo a ti, ningún cuchillo en este mundo podría quebrar nuestro amor.

(*Believe me, every day I love you more and on July 25, I'll only let you down if I am dead.* [Can you believe that? only if he's dead]. *I truly love you with all of my heart, and if it weren't a sin, I'd love you more than God himself.* [more than God, imagine that] *If you loved me as much as I love you, no knife could destroy our love.*)

Isn't that wonderful, to love each other so much and be able to say it; that's what's difficult. You, for example, never tell me things like that; I think it's because nowadays we express our feelings physically and back then they only had recourse to words. Can you imagine how hard their love must have been, being cousins and all? In another letter, complete with spelling mistakes (because by that time all schooling was in English and our people didn't learn to write their native language correctly, they just wrote words as they said them), he tells her:

> *Vida, dices que el padre nos casa como le dé la gana por eso no ay cuidau, que el padre pagándole no le importa si todos los días se casan primos hermanos y no ay diferencia.*

> *(Sweetheart, you say the priest will marry us if he feels like it, so not to worry; as long as he gets paid, the priest doesn't care if first cousins get married every day,* [I knew you would like that part] *so it's not a problem.)*

Yes, that's what he said. I learned them by heart because they're so beautiful and I wanted them to be a part of me. Well it appears that it **was** a problem and they had to get permission from the Bishop. What we discovered after my grandmother's death, when we found the letters, was that they didn't get married in July, but several months later, and their first daughter was born five months after they were married, can you believe that? I suspect they were denied permission to marry, so they forced things by getting her pregnant. Then what could the family say, because it was a well-known and respected family in that area; it was embarrassing enough that these two little cousins had fallen in love, but when she ended up pregnant they must have had to pay plenty so everything could be done respectably. So my dear, it should be quite clear to you that promiscuity flows in my blood.

You were quiet, so I kept on insisting, and how about you, do you love me as much as my grandfather loved my grandmother? Would you sacrifice your honor and your life for me? Don't tell me, I already know what you're going to say, that you would make that sacrifice only for the class struggle. And by the way, Sergio, just in case you've contemplated it, don't even think of getting me pregnant, because for my generation there's still the danger of having a baby with a pig's tail —on account of my grandparents' sin, of course.

My parents, though, were not cousins, even though they did have the same last name. So I'm Martínez on my paternal grandfather's side, on my paternal grandmother's side and on my maternal grandfather's side. But even though they weren't cousins they played together and loved each other since they were children, and when they were twenty-eight they eloped. My father's father almost had a heart attack, since he considered my mother way too inferior for his son. It's incredible that my mamá agreed to a clandestine marriage, because she always suffered from an illness called *"el qué dirán"*, that insipid fear of being tried in the court of public opinion.

Now I believe that she is truly an admirable woman, despite the fact that on the surface she appears so ordinary. I remember when she was still quite young, and would spend the whole day singing and working her heart out, just like my father: in the garden, in the corral, or even roofing the house. She had been a teacher before that and later went back to teaching, and that alone is beyond the ordinary given the social conditions of those times. She was from a poor family; her father died when she was seven years old and her mother had to resort to cleaning houses for Anglos, and washing and ironing their clothes. Mamá used to tell us about how they lived at the edge of town in a little shanty, with wooden planks for a floor; between the cracks they could see snakes that lived under the house and every morning her mother would pour boiling water over them.

They covered the walls with newspapers and as she learned to read, she would sound out the words of the newspaper articles to entertain her younger siblings. When she started school she only knew Spanish, but since the children weren't allowed to speak their native language, they quickly learned English, although it was a bit choppy at first. When she was in the third grade she had a teacher that played the piano and who treated her with a great deal of tenderness. That's when, can you believe this Sergio, at the age of eight, my mamá decided that she was going to be a teacher when she grew up, and play the piano. Yes, that same child who from her bed could see snakes slithering under the floorboards of her house. Well, when she was seventeen years old and had just finished high school, she was offered a job as a teacher in a village two hundred miles from her home. She accepted it because she saw it as an opportunity to free her mother from washing floors on her hands and knees. When she said good-bye to my father she didn't let him kiss her because she believed that was something that should only happen between married people. She was so innocent that when she began her period, she became so frightened that she threw herself down in the irrigation ditch and stayed there all day long, until my grandmother finally went in and dragged her out. And there she was, just imagine, alone and with all her innocence, heading for what must have seemed to her like the edge of the world, to make a living.

During the next ten years she was a teacher in a rural school where she taught reading and writing to children, some of whom were almost her age when she first started to work. I can just picture her now, small and timid, but with an incredible inner strength, whipping overgrown boys who misbehaved in her classroom. She bought a used piano but only learned to play "*Las cuatro milpas.*" Even now she sits at her antique piano and plays the only song in her repertoire; her eyes light up as if she were seeing her whole life unfold before her like a movie in slow motion. I think as she plays she feels that besides her five daughters, her song is the only thing in the world that really belongs to her. Well, the song and her abiding faith in the Virgin Mary.

After getting married they went to live at a ranch owned by my father's aunt and uncle, the ones who had raised him. Even today they talk about that period of their lives as the time they lived in their own heaven on earth.

During the war they lost the ranch and went to live in town and after that in Mexico for two years. This was when the US government was recruiting Mexican ranchers from the Southwest to go work with the AFTOSA. I think this is the only time it officially recognized the value of the language of Chicanos. Of course, all the directors and bosses of the U.S. team were white and the peons "Mexican-American," but without the latter they would never have gained entry to the Mexican villages to vaccinate the cattle. My papá, for example, would arrive at a small village like Tala, and head directly to the parish house to explain his mission to the priest. On Sunday he went to mass and the priest would introduce him to the parish, urging them to cooperate with him. On Monday they would begin vaccinating the villagers' cows and goats and from there they went on to the ranches.

When we returned from Mexico, Papá got sick and couldn't find work for some time. Mamá went back to teaching and that was what she did until she retired some years ago. In a way, Mamá has always been an enigma to me. I always perceived her to be so emotionally dependent on my father and at the same time I know she had a tremendous will and interior strength. All her life she was haunted by fears and doubts; however, she learned to function in a foreign and hostile environment (I mean the Gringos' environment) and that was the legacy she left us. Nonetheless, my sisters and I were always crazy about Papá. We competed aggressively for his attention, each wanting to be the son he never had. And we just ignored Mamá. It was natural for her to do all the housework as well as perform her outside job, and she did it so we could have new dresses and shoes for Christmas and some day she could send us to the university. Now that I reflect on my family's life, I see my mother as an imposing and stable rock that emerges from the earth and imposes itself heroically across the landscape of my life.

Oh, do forgive me, my love, for boring you with all this. It's just that I had a nostalgia attack. Besides, I want to be an open book for you. I don't know why, but I have this urgent need to tell you all the details of my life.

LADIES AND GENTLEMEN, may I please have your attention. You have the marvelous fortune of traveling on this train at this precise moment, for I carry in this case a true bargain. My dearest ladies and gentlemen, this may be the deal of your lifetime. These pictures of Our Crucified Lord are of the finest quality that has ever been presented on the public market. I have just obtained them in the United States, where they adorn the most beautiful and modern churches in that country. Notice, dear friends, the beautiful details, the perfect countenance of our Lord and Master. Observe his eyes. Don't they reflect the most pure and perfect love? How many will you take? Fifteen *pesos* each. Don't miss this unique opportunity. I have only twenty left, the last twenty that exist in the world. They've sold out in the States and in Mexico you will only find these that your humble servant now offers you. Señor, will you take one? Señorita, how many for you? Don't miss your chance to buy this beautiful picture of Our Redeemer, so that He may adorn and bless your humble home.

When did we last see each other? Was it only four days ago? I can't believe it. You know, when one day goes by without seeing you, I miss you so much I want to die. Has it really been only four days? It seemed so much longer. But you know I also like it when we don't see each other for a while because then my orgasms are always so incredibly intense. I don't know, they seem to last longer. Today for example, it was just incredible, like a flood of electrically charged waves. I thought it would never end. Can you imagine what it would be like to get stuck in a perpetual orgasm? It would be something like when you can't stop sneezing —pleasure and agony. In strictly biological terms, sneezing is like an orgasm, don't you think? I, for example, love to sneeze. I feel this great satisfaction and pleasure when I do.

You know the first one, the first orgasm I mean, is always fantastic, isn't it? That's because it's the discharge of a tremendous accumulation of energy, but in no way does it come near the intensity and satisfaction of the second or third. I don't know exactly how to explain it but these seem to come from a much deeper place than the first, especially if they come close together. Sometimes I feel like they spring forth from the very center of my physical and spiritual being. Don't laugh. I don't know how else to explain it. It's really impossible to describe the feeling but, *sans doute*, it's worth the effort, even though it's so hard to find the right words. Tell me the truth, aren't you just a little bit jealous because I can have a whole series of orgasms without having to wait to recuperate from the first one? The other night Toña, Lupe, Isaura and I were talking, and we decided that patriarchy owes its existence to the female multiple orgasm. Yes, I'm serious.

Look, if the female is capable of having multiple

La puta

orgasms, what's going to keep her from taking off with another man while the first one recovers? Of course, afterwards there would be a big mess regarding paternity —but that's another story. So you see it more as a question of inheritance of private property? Well, I know that, but that doesn't diminish the possibility that there actually exists a relationship between the social position (not to mention their supine position during the conjugal act) of women and their propensity for multiple orgasms.

Listen up, I think when man, Adam or whoever it was, realized that women had this special talent, it dawned on him how difficult it would be to control his beloved Eve. (Perhaps you're right, and it was dear Sigmund, but I imagine that this information was already floating around during Adam's tenure on earth.) *Caramba*, the ungrateful wench might even run off with that damned serpent. So what could he do? My own idea, and this is purely a personal interpretation, is that there were only two solutions, the first one being to deny her those multiple orgasms, making her believe that the only genuine orgasm was the orgasm produced by the masculine organ injected in the female receptacle.

Now, if she were not satisfied, and given that he had to recuperate, was it not possible to permit unorthodox methods (nimble fingers, articulate tongues, etc.)? Absolutely not, because this would give her the idea that her pleasure did not depend on you-know-what... on the sacred instrument. It followed that any woman dissatisfied with one lone orgasm, and we're talking of course of one brought about through coitus, *non erat mulierem integram*. Now, since there was always the chance someone would rebel, some chick inclined to pursue more, to pursue variety, it became necessary to brand her in some way, to stigmatize her —you got it babe, for her orgasmic gluttony— before the whole world.

So here comes solution number two: coin a denigrating and accusing noun. (To stand for what? Well, for the female addicted to the pleasure of multiple orgasms). **Right on**, Bucko! LA PUTA. With that little

four-letter word, together with the myth of the exclusive
orgasm —of the penis- (preferably the husband's)-in-the-
vagina type— little Eve's lascivious behavior was brought
under control and dear Adam was left free to play Don
Juan. We could add to this analysis a comment on the
phenomenon that there does not exist a female version
of the word cuckold. That is to say that the woman who
has more than one man is said to turn her husband into
a cuckold, an unforgivable and infinitely embarrassing
condition for the cuckolded victim. However, the male
who has extracurricular women neither cuckolds nor
stigmatizes in any other fashion his wife or partner; *au
contraire*, he is praised for being a real man, while his
wife will one day (specifically at her husband's wake) be
proclaimed a saint.

Furthermore, we could also note that alongside this
curious cultural/linguistic phenomenon, there exists
another no less curious one; to wit: there is no masculine
equivalent for nymphomaniac. Oh sure, I thought you'd
bring up "satyr." But have you ever heard, in a simple
daily conversation, the most lascivious man in the given
universe of discourse referred to as a satyr? Now tell me,
how many nymphomaniacs do you know? At least 139.
Oh dude, I love the way you complement my speeches!
You're a great straight man. So to sum up: woman given
to promiscuity = puta, nymphomaniac and cuckolder
(or is it cockholder?). All of them negative and accusing
signs. On the other hand, a male cut from the same cloth
is applauded and held as a cultural idol.

You're right, I have gone off on a bit of a tangent.
Nonetheless, it's all relevant. Now, the only thing left for
me to say regarding this topic is that what women need
to do is explore and develop the multiple orgasm and
make it the basis for a new political ideology. I should
have known. You love the idea, because there is nothing
you enjoy more than facilitating my reaching as many
orgasms as I desire, in any way or form, with or without
a penis. And are you sure you don't suffer from just a
teeny-tiny inferiority complex in this terrain? Oh, Sergio,
forsooth! thou art a jewel.

A-laaaaaaaaaaaaaar-ma! Oh, pardon me, Señorita, don't be alarmed. I'm just selling the magazine *Alarma*. You will buy a copy, won't you? Come on, it'll make your trip less boring. Look at these headlines: TWO-HEADED CREATURE BORN IN JOJUTLA. Oh boy, if that isn't something. And here, look at this one: COCAINE ROTS RICHARD BURTON'S NOSE. Can you believe that? They'll just have to give him an artificial nose, won't they? And look, this ought to interest you, being a Pocha and all: NORTH AMERICAN HIPPIES CAUSE DRUG INCREASE IN MEXICO CITY. And check this photo out: what a bod! Shut your mouth, you rude bastard, and let me have one. Thank you, Señorita, you won't regret it.

...Well now, this erudite reading calls for a good Mexican cigarette and the peace and quiet of my berth. I'll see if I can sleep after reading this yellow-sheet tabloid...

...Dear God. Who's knocking at my door at this hour? It must be Lencho. What a stubborn dude. Just because we spoke a bit —well, the truth is we had a long and interesting conversation at suppertime and he isn't as dense as I imagined him to be— he thinks I'm his sweetheart...

Who is it?

It's me, Lencho. Please open up, just for a moment. I need you to do me a favor.

...A favor, jeez, nothing like resorting to euphemisms....

It's late, Lencho, and I want to sleep.

Please, Pochita. It's really important.

...Well, he was nice enough to fix the toilet after our stop at Aguascalientes, in spite of the fact that he had a bunch of other things to do. Truth is I owe him one, but if this brute attacks me, first I'll poke his eyes and then I'll slam my knee into his you-know-what....

For God's sake, what do you want at this hour?

Listen, Pochita, could you please hide this little box in your berth until morning? I'll pick it up when we get to Mexico City.

No way. I'm not hiding who-knows-what crap in my berth. Why don't you hide it in yours?

I can't, because the boss goes through all our stuff. Come on, don't make me beg. It's only a little gift from the border that I bought for my girlfriend. If the boss finds it, he'll take it and give it to his old lady.

All right, leave it and make yourself scarce, because if I don't sleep a couple of hours tonight I'll look like hell when we arrive in the morning.

No way we can let that happen, *verdad*, Pochita? You've got to look your best so all those Mexico City boys will fall for you. Right? I'm warning you, they're all a bunch of fags so don't get your hopes too high. If its men you want, *amorcito*, you can't beat the ones from Chihuahua. But you'll have to find that out on your own.

Don't think I haven't noticed that you *Shi*huahua guys think you're Pancho Villa. Well, in case you don't know it ,dude, Pancho Villa is old news these days. Cowboys are out of style. Don't you know we have another Latin Hero? If you must know, his name is Che. But what would you know, *armadillo del desierto*?

Oh, you've got some spark, Pochita! I can feel the blood rushing to my...heart!...when you talk like that. What a pity you're not like the blondies from the other side. If you were, for sure there'd be a good time happenin' in this cabin tonight!

Lencho, why don't you try this on for size (obscene gesture), it might just fit you to a T. (She slams the door shut.)

...A gift for his girlfriend, yeah, right. He must think I'm retarded or something. I wonder what it is? Of course, they're pornographic magazines and paraphernalia. Perhaps it's a gun and this cretin is planning to kill and dismember me, then throw the pieces out the window —first a foot, then the left ear, a handful of hair, the right arm. DAMN IT! WILL YOU STOP?!

'Tis obvious, *querida*, that they're drugs and fool that you are, you've agreed to be his mule. I wouldn't be surprised if upon arriving in Mexico City, he asked you to deliver the box to his girlfriend because he didn't get the days off they'd promised him and he's got to leave in ten minutes on the outbound for Juárez. Do you have any idea what they'd do to you if the police caught you with drugs? That's right, you'd be off to Lecumberri to rot with all those pothead hippies. Ooooh, the calls to your parents, if you send us ten thousand dollars we'll set her free, then five thousand more, then afterwards, I'm sorry but we just can't do it, you'll have to come yourselves to do all the paper work, and months will turn into years and each day you'll get another gray hair, and the guards will play lascivious games with your body whenever they please, and one transparent winter day, one of those that happens only where the air is clear, they'll find you in a stiff little ball with your lungs rotted out (from the humidity in your cell, and not as a result of those nasty cigarettes that you had to quit smoking long ago when you ran out of money).

Dear Pocho Parents From the Other Side:

We regret having to inform you by means of this letter that your daughter, the precious Pochita who spent ten years in Lecumberri, has died from tuberculosis...

Jeez, who the hell is knocking again at this hour?

¿Quién es?

Señorita, please open the door. I have a message from Lencho. He says to give me the box.

Are you crazy, or have your screws shaken loose from the vibrations of the train?

No, nothing like that, Señorita. Lencho says that it's very important that you give it to me.

Okay, take it, and tell him not to bother me again with that damn box. I NEED TO SLEEP!

...Oh, God, these Mexican cigarettes smell like horseshit, ugh, and they taste worse than horseshit. Well, I'll just have to learn to like them. I wonder what these poor fools are up to, here's the box, there's the box, now the box is gone. I wonder when they'll show up with a hat and fluffy white rabbits. Oh well, I'm so sleepy that I don't give a damn...

...The train comes to a halt at the edge of a promontory that points toward the center of an enormous lake. She looks out the window and in the distance sees a city that seems suspended above the very heart of the lake. She dresses hastily, grabs her bags and abandons her berth. In the passageway she runs into Lencho, who extends his arms to keep her from passing. She turns quickly to run in the opposite direction but Lencho's octopus arms quickly wrap around her waist, as he presses his lips to her ear and begs her to stay on the train while the other passengers get off. His breath is a burning flame that envelops her in a hypnotic trance. His dexterous hands slide beneath her red sweater and his erect penis assails her buttocks like a blind man's cane seeking the entrance to an unfamiliar building. She feels a glob of lubricant descend and instinctively begins to weave her hips around in a slow and deliberate rhythm against the huge rigid organ that demands entry. Suddenly she remembers that the train has reached its destination and she thinks surely they must be in Mexico City. She slides like soft jello through Lencho's arms and with erect nipples pointing the way she runs toward the sleeping-car door.

The morning light blinds her sleepless eyes and she almost slips on the step. When she finally recovers her normal vision she begins to see the movement of a beautiful and intricate human kaleidoscope that unfolds in an improvised dance along the wide and clean streets. Hundreds of barefoot youth wearing loincloths that barely cover their private parts glide like Olympic skaters along the walkway, offering rental canoes and litters to the recent arrivals. Girls with black braids tied with rainbow-colored ribbons, dressed in white huipiles, announce their merchandise in singsong chants:

*mangoes, pineapples, yams, roasted corn on the cob,
and anything else the tired traveler might desire. She
proceeds slowly, opening a swath through the crowd of
people that pulsates around her to the beat of an interior
drum. The smells of the street — spoiling fruit, singed
corn husks, scurrying bodies— assault her nose and she
feels a strong urge to vomit.*

*Suddenly two midgets hold their ground before
her, both wearing white loincloths and green and pink
waistbands. They inform her that their señora has sent
them to receive her; they invite her to board a canopied
canoe adorned with green and gold embroidered
plumes. Awed by the carnival that undulates before her
eyes, which until the moment of stepping off the train
had lived in the most abject sensual deprivation, she
silently obeys. She has no idea where the jolly midgets
are taking her, but she feels compelled by an unknown
force to go with them.*

*They travel several hours by canoe along a raised
causeway that links the promontory to the distant city,
whose impressive towers and stone buildings glitter
under a tropical sun. Upon reaching the main island, the
canoe passes through one of many narrow canals that
cross the city like liquid sidewalks, and at whose banks
stand one- and two-story homes of red tezontli and
painted adobe, each with a lush garden on the roof. With
every oar stroke they draw nearer to the white teocallis
that rise like mirages of temples against an enormous,
translucent background of blue. Dumbfounded, she
looks all around, thinking that what spreads out
before her "is a dream," because she "sees things never
imagined or seen before, nor even dreamed."*

*But it is not a dream, as revealed by her delicate
sense of smell that discerns the aroma of thick layers
of putrefied blood covering the stairways of the sacred
temples. As if this were not disconcerting enough to
the newcomer, there appears in her field of vision an
enormous abacus whose hundreds of beads consist
of grotesque skulls aligned on bamboo stakes like
sinister gargoyles on silent and somber guard. For the*

*second time that morning she feels like emptying the
contents of her stomach through her mouth. As quickly
as this physical reaction appears, it vanishes and she
concentrates her attention on the scene that slowly and
marvelously unfolds before her eyes as the canoe passes
through an archway carved in the wall which she will
soon learn encloses one of the castles of the Great Lord
of Tenochtitlan. The canoe floats into an enormous
garden that rests quietly between the four walls of the
magnificent castle. She steps out of the canoe and before
her stands a woman whose noble aspect is revealed by
her dress and her regal presence.⁴*

4   Doña Marina was at this time in the morning of life.
She is said to have possessed uncommon personal attractions (see poem below) and her open, expressive features
indicated her generous temper. She always remained faithful
to the countrymen of her adoption; and her knowledge and
customs of the Mexicans, and often of their designs, enabled
her to extricate Spaniards, more than once, from the most
embarrassing and perilous situations. She had her errors,
as we have seen. But they should be rather charged to the
defects of early education, and to the evil influence of him to
whom in the darkness of her spirit she looked with simple
confidence for the light to guide her. All agree that she was
full of excellent qualities, and the important services which
she rendered the Spaniards have made her memory deservedly dear to them; while the name of Malinche—the name
by which she is still known in Mexico—was pronounced with
kindness by the conquered races, with whose misfortunes
she showed an invariable sympathy:

> Admire tan lúcida cabalgada
> Y espéctaculo Doña Marina
> India Noble al caudillo presentada,
> De fortuna y belleza peregrina
>
> Con despejado espíritu y viveza
> Gira la vista en el concurso mudo;
> Rico manto de extrema sutileza

How beautiful you are! she proclaims enthusiastically. I have been very conscious that my behavior would produce a strong and handsome people. Seeing you pleases me a great deal and compensates me for the insults and the tongue-lashings that history will pile upon me.[3]

Taking her by the arm, she leads Mari on a walk through the garden. The noble lady continues pronouncing a long discourse in a voice, now serene, that contrasts sharply with the content of her message.

Mari, you have had the good fortune of arriving before the imminent destruction of this magnificent city. Of all that you have seen today —the temples, the marketplaces, the palaces, this garden— only testimonial ashes will remain. These foreigners that have been sent by our gods are a destructive plague. Though they are few in comparison to the extension of our nation, their triumph is inexorable. Even if our great Lord were in condition to act decisively and we could hold back this voracious wave of fire-spitting men, more would come, and even more, and finally hordes of them would arrive to brutally pick the last flower of our race, sending each and every one of us to rest in the darkness of Mictlan. The end of our world as we know it is inevitable; nonetheless it is possible and imperative that we save what we can. Ours is a beautiful race, strong and prolific. Nonetheless, there are those among us who are doing their best to destroy it through internecine strife; we are trapped and fixed in the circle of time because of constant battles, hunger for iniquitous power, and the desire to maintain this level of opulence. If our plumed mud-eaters from the provinces did not

Con chapas de oro autorizarla pudo,

Prendido con bizarra gentileza
Sobre los pechos en ayroso nudo;
Reyna parece de la Indiana Zona,
Varonil y hermosísima Amazona.

produce such plentiful food and goods with the sweat
of their back, if they did not extract valuable resources
from our mother earth, it would not be possible for the
distinguished eagles and jaguars to live as they do; and
to ensure this order they must divide and conquer, they
must impose perpetual and flowery warfare.

And now these false gods will take advantage of our
discord to defeat us. It is painful to say, Mari, but our
leaders are weak, either of body or of mind. Some want
to resist in order to salvage the moment; those are the
weak of mind because they do not understand that this
will provoke the ire and voracity of these barbarians.
Prince Cuauhtémoc, for example, will resist even as
they burn his feet and future mythmakers will pay him
homage and build monuments in his honor, but what
historians will not admit is that even if Falling Eagle
were to prevail, his triumph would be momentary
because it wouldn't be long before the King from across
the sea would send every last one of his vassals to
destroy our people.

It seems that the kingdom of that cacique don
Fernando is in dire straits. His people find themselves
in a state of deep anxiety. They are overwhelmed by the
knowledge that they are headed down the path of no
return. They are trapped in worn-out models and their
ancient myths are losing their cosmic significance. They
search everywhere for an escape from the abyss that
engulfs them and they look to our world for salvation.
The fact that they come burdened with profound doubts
will force them to destroy our world...with the sword,
cross, and phallus. And Moctezuma, my poor Lord of
the Crooked Staff, has his balls in a vise, manipulated
by the priests with their magic and superstition; he
has the noblest soul that has ever walked this earth,
but he is weak, and his fear of the gods will force him
to collaborate with these beasts. But listen carefully,
Mari, I want you to understand our situation so that
some day, when you feel wounded by the violence of the
words, "son of the chingada whore," you will understand
the motives that compel my actions. Let me begin with

the fact that women in this society, just as they will be in yours, are mere objects, they are chattel, they are the property first of their fathers, then of their spouses. The only honor that they are granted in this culture is to be sacrificed while they are still virgins. Some honor!

All the important people —the priests, the nobles, the merchants, the artisans, the warriors— are males. We women are first and foremost the mirrors that reflect the male's image so that he can know who he is; beyond that, we are his plaything in bed, and finally, we are receptacles and incubators for his kernels of maize. We are relegated to the world of shadows and silence; but that silence engenders the word that laps up our bile and becomes rancor, curses, and also song; and to this word another is added and another and another and in the end they form one long, sturdy chain that envelops and strangles us. We can render ourselves impotent before this chain, expire asphyxiated by words that never found a voice, or we can conjure up that voice, with all the signs of heaven and hell, and turn it back on the world of the great lords. Before our voice, they will recoil in fear and they will show their true tendencies: solitude, reticence that hides behind masks, and sexual organs that fire away like bows and arrows, like muskets and shotguns. Can you imagine, Mari, if we could bring together the chains of words of each and every woman of the world, the power we could generate? And we could direct that power toward the creation of a society where all could wander unclothed, without shame, without lies or weaknesses to hide; a society where the fruits of labor and of our mother earth would be divided equally; a society where all men and women would take charge of nurturing and educating our daughters and sons so they could learn to act graciously, with honor, creativity, and human compassion. We women are strong, Mari, but our strength is often hidden, resulting from the silence imposed by social and legal maneuvers that have gagged our mouths.

— Consequently, I find myself at the crossroads of a treacherous path. I am burdened by a history of infamy and degradation. *Not only once, but twice have I been sold like a common object, first by my mother and the second time like a chunk of flesh, by my lord who, in exchange, hoped to receive the good favor of Cortés. Ah yes, Cortés. We finally reach the topic of my bowlegged lover, that beast of the white gods, astute brandisher of the sword, master of the game of manipulation, persistent seeker of glory and fame.*

From the beginning I saw in his eyes that spark that compels human beings to commit the most desperate acts on their path of ascendancy. Everywhere I could see our caciques vacillate before him, he was definitely a god, no, he wasn't a god, perhaps he was a god after all. I decided to put an end to their doubts. I lay with him and discovered that he makes love like any mortal man, precipitously and anguished by the limitations of his instrument. And I have also discovered his proclivity toward power. I have decided to become his ally so that I may absorb the power that surely will be his, and thus alter the destiny of my people, who find themselves marching toward annihilation. I make use of the power of my voice and I offer it to Cortés, thus becoming his tongue and his go-between. Yes, the necessary link between his world and ours. My objective is to help him further his imperious designs through words and compromise. I see this as the only path to the salvation of our nation, and that is what most obsesses me at this crucial moment. Because of me many have died, in Cholula thousands of brave warriors perished, and many more will die before this has ended.

But in the end, if my collaboration with this spell-casting devil is necessary to assure that not every one of us dies, I am willing to sell myself. I have been sold before, after all, but in this case my sale is the result of the exercise of my free will, which does not allow me to acquiesce passively to the total destruction of my people. My act of treason, for that is how history will brand it, promises to insert the seed of our flower in the new order that inexorably will spread in the directions of the four winds. Without my act of collaboration, our people would disappear and all that would be left in this land would be the rarefied race of these false lords, weak and anemic before the enormity, the majesty, and the unpredictable nature of our environment. Nonetheless, because of my actions, a new mestizo race will be born in whose veins will flow the strength of my blood, my will, my woman's word. You, Mari, are the future fruit of my womb, the flower of my betrayal.

Internal or external observer, I, you, she, Mari. How does one narrate a dream? Is the dreamer the narrator? Is she the cinematographer? Is she also the dreamed? The actress? The dreamer stands outside looking at the dream. Then she sees herself, so she is also inside. She is both outside and inside. From without, she perceives the action visually like an omniscient observer. From within, she feels observed from the outside by herself. She feels far away, distanced from what is being dreamed; but she also feels near, emotionally linked to the action. What difference is there between the dream and narration?

Señorita, open up. This is Captain Acevedo speaking. Open the door. Señorita, open up, please. We don't have all night.

....Oh, God. Who's knocking at two in the morning? Don't tell me they're bringing back the damn box....

Go to hell, Lencho, and let me sleep.

Perdón, señorita, that we've forced our way in like this, but we have to check all the berths. Could you step into the hall, please?

What are you doing? How dare you...

Señorita, your best bet is to keep that sweet painted mouth of yours shut and do what I say. That way we won't have any complaints later about broken arms and such, if you know what I mean.

...Is this guy for real? Is this damn trip for real? Maybe I'm really a character in an Agatha Christie script, riding the Orient Express and don't even know it. Jesus, that imbecile is going through my stuff as if he owned it...

Gracias, señorita, and forgive us for bothering you. You can go back to sleep now. *Buenas noches.*

....Oh, isn't he hilarious, go back to sleep, sweetie. Where are those damn cigarettes? And what's this all about? I know they've had problems with the peasant uprisings, and the army has had to intervene, but that's in the mountains. Besides, these jerks were looking for something —something specific. Lencho's damn box! That must be it. I wonder what the story is. I can't wait to hear what he'll have to say tomorrow. For now, I have no choice but to smoke these cancer sticks...

He lay there for a long, long time, his face glued to the cold steel, his hands grasping the metal bar that ran along the side of the roof. He felt a strong urge to roll over so he could gaze at the thousands of stars sparkling against the black dome that covered the desert, but the fear of discovery forced him to remain face down, paralyzed in a precarious position, his muscles cramping and his lungs struggling to breathe the rushing air.

...Damn pigs, it's taking them long enough. I can just see them searching every inch of the train, even the toilet. Thank God we took it out of the Pochita's berth. I don't know what I was thinking, putting her in such danger. That chick's something else. She thinks she's so tough but she's just hiding behind a heavy mask because she doesn't know who she is. But who the hell would know, living in limbo, trapped between two worlds, as Pochos do. Mexico forgot all about them a long time ago, and they're still hanging on, clinging to the fringes. No matter how hard they try to be like the Gringos, they're always outside the wall of illusion looking in, with the sad eyes of a hungry child at the window of a candy shop. Sometimes I think that even the hapless illegals who cross over have it better. At least they know who they are: worker ants, thankful for any breadcrumbs, because in the end it's bread in their kids' bellies, that's what matters. They don't even go near the wall of illusion. If they don't learn English, who cares, people everywhere speak Spanish. If they don't educate their children, who cares; since when is education going to create a little opening in the great wall of illusion? The few gaps that do exist are reserved for the more astute Pochos, those who have forgotten their native language, who in a minute would do a cartwheel or whatever else is asked of them, to prove they deserve to exist within the magic circle.

I think that's why the Pochita is on her way to Mexico City. The fear of being siphoned through a tiny crack into the vacuous circle compels her to return to her roots in search of the smallest seed of identity. Poor little Pocha, is she in for a surprise when she rams into the other wall of illusion. I longed to tell her once and for all that Mexicans don't give a damn about *la otra cara de México,* the so-called other face of Mexico. The Pochos are over there because they're a bunch of yellow-bellied traitors, and that's all there is to it. If they have a hard time of it, well that's their problem; who the hell tells them to go suffer over there, to expose themselves to the Gringo's kicks in the ass and spit in the face. It's better to suffer in one's own hut than in someone else's palace. But there's no way to convince them of that; they deserve what they get, those scratchbacks, wetbacks, Rio Grande surfers, wets, tonks, aliens, fools, traitors. And the ones Santa Anna sold out —Mexicans don't know a damn thing about them. They think they all turned into Gringos the moment the Treaty of Guadalupe Hidalgo was signed. As far as they're concerned, the only Mexican who exists on the other side is a damned Malinchista.

But I didn't dare mention all of this to la Pochita so as not to destroy the innocent illusion that compels her to travel to this shitty country that every day buries its progeny with bellies swollen from hunger, and worse yet, pushes them, *chale,* kicks them all the way to the elusive dorado. All I could do was bite my tongue and play the role of the asshole macho, the way we do with the Gringas, trying in that way to seek vengeance against who knows what, perhaps against the foreign master who sucks our blood and leaves us lying naked so that afterwards our own bosses can castrate us like goddamned animals —I'm your master, you son of a bitch, and that's why I'm leaving you with only the balls that you yourself can invent (and the bigger the better, because those are the ones bitches and queers like to suck). So we don masks to cover the impotence that allows us no other way out of this damn labyrinth of fat politicians, shrinking pesos, and ghosts of our glorious and blood-drenched past.

And this Pochita —whom I was forced to use because in this life, as Fuentes once said, those who don't fuck first are fucked over— how I would love to wrap her in velvet caresses to protect her from the kicks in the ass and spit in the face that her grandparents' motherland will no doubt shower upon her, merely for being the product of a vile historical act that has given birth to a chain of immutable and multiple iniquities.

Chingao, this cold wind is beating me senseless. I can't feel my feet, and my hands are like claws, I'm sure rigor mortis has set in. Just how much time do they need to find and destroy the dream of one poor fool? I'm just someone who counts less than a grain of sand in this enormous desert. And where is everybody? Where are the lights? Not even a hovel lit up by the quivering flame of a candle! This unending blackness is interrupted only by a fragile steel rail –the connection between two circles of hell— with a rickety train and a godforsaken Mexican, *un pobre pendejo,* trapped between the train and the dark night while some sons of bitches search for an accursed little box...

So how, you have probably asked yourselves, did she know what Lencho was thinking during those perilous moments? The truth is that this passage, for reasons you will eventually discover, I had to invent, that is to say, I imagined it. Now that you know this, somebody out there is sure to accuse me of having been too accommodating, for portraying him in such a positive light. Let me assure you, not for one moment did I doubt that his intentions were irredeemably sexist and that, in fact, he was motivated by a strong desire to get into my pants. However, I always felt an inexplicable need to remember him in another way.

What's up, love. Did you get tired of waiting? I
dropped by the bookstore and they told me you were
out. Afterwards, I stopped to buy a record. Look, it's
Victor Jara's new album. Come here, tell me what you did
today. Me? Well, I had a really interesting day. First, as
usual, I went to my classes, then to Casa Aztlán, where I
got lost in hours and hours of conversation. Afterwards,
Luis and I decided to take a walk downtown. I think we
were a bit bored and wanted to see if we could find any
action. From downtown we decided to walk over to the
Plaza de las Tres Culturas. Do you remember that I once
asked you to take me there and we headed that way but
never got there? We ran into some of your friends and
they invited us to coffee so we never went. Remember?
Well, I never gave up on going there, and today I went
with Luis.

We went into the chapel and it was there that our
little adventure began to unfold. I was sitting in a pew,
just taking it all in. Luis began to walk around looking
at everything with a strange intensity, but I just ignored
him. After a while, I saw him standing before the altar.
You know how there are some lava stones that form the
altar. Well, Luis began to touch them and to walk from
one to another. Then I noticed that he began to stroke
them as if they were precious gems. I began to observe
him carefully because I had a peculiar sensation that
something was wrong. That's when he began to cry,
and rub his body against the rock. Of course I became
frightened, and rushed over to him.

What's wrong? What's going on?, and he wouldn't
answer me. It was as if I weren't there, and he kept on
moving from stone to stone like a madman, trying to
squeeze something from them that I couldn't possibly
know, and all that time the tears were streaming down

his face. I noticed everybody was looking at him and whispering, so I took him by the hand and led him outdoors. By then he was shaking and wailing and crying like a baby. And I'm thinking, this dude took something, mushrooms or peyote or something stronger. You know how we're always talking about how we're going to experiment with mushrooms, but never do. Anyway, I couldn't calm him down and everyone was staring at us like we were the afternoon's entertainment, but a few came over to offer help. After a while he started to get some kind of convulsions all over his body and I didn't know what to do, whether to take him to the hospital or what.

Finally I managed to sit him on a step in the plaza. I took him in my arms and began to rock him. It was purely instinctual to rock him and caress his face and hair, and hum to him as if he were an infant. Gradually he began to calm down, and finally he sat up and said let's get out of here. We walked several blocks without saying a word. Yes, in absolute silence. Then we went into a small bar and I ordered two beers, and he still remained mute. We sat quietly for a long while and finally he told me, I don't know what it is about that place but I felt these incredible vibes —a sensation that engulfed and suffocated me. Then I began to see a series of visions, faces distorted by pain, bodies fleeing, blood flowing, and I thought I heard shouts echoing in the air. I don't know, Mari, really I don't know what happened to me in there. I've never experienced anything like that before, but it was as real as the liquid in this glass. He was still pale and his hands trembled as he raised a cigarette to his mouth.

You know, Sergio, that Luis is not a scandalous or frivolous young man. He is very serious, super-sensitive to be sure, maybe even hyper-sensitive. Well, of course I was frightened, Sergio. Hey, what's wrong? Why'd you turn your back on me? Oh no, not you, too. What is this, Cry-Baby Day? What's going on, Sergio? Tell me. What's wrong, my love? Please, Sergio, tell me, what's happening to you? Why are you crying?

No time like the present to ask you (myself), why the trip to Mexico. The flight from Steve is obvious and even appropriate, but this bit about recovering your childhood is really dumb. Childhood is never recuperated; it comes to an end: poof, it's gone; it ceases to exist. Whatever was good or bad about it is deep within you and that's all that remains: a few memories and a mess of feelings, fears, hopes, prejudices, ambivalent and contradictory attitudes, all of which are you. So let's try another tack here, why are you really going to Mexicles?

Okay, perhaps there is some basis for the idea that you're going in search of your past, not your personal past but rather a history, or better said, a pre-history which atavistically beckons and obsesses you with the need to encounter it head on. A return to the distant root, to the seed, retracing lost steps in order to discover something that might help you defend yourself against the rushing waters that every day drag you along more forcefully, threatening to shatter your very essence into splinters. But tell me, what does your reality have to do with Mexico? Well for starters, you (that is to say, we) New Mexicans need to search for our roots in our homeland.

It's obvious that the Spaniards imposed their institutions, their language, their cultural values on New Mexico and it is precisely these that link us to the rest of the Hispanic world. Nevertheless, the indigenous element must be searched for within the Southwest and in the cultures of this region, because just as there developed a mestizo culture in Mexico, a similar one developed in the Rio Grande Valley, but the autochthonous element differed from Mexico's, Peru's, or Bolivia's. While in Mexico there evolved a new Mexican culture, in your land there developed a new New Mexican culture. Well, I suppose you're right (that is, I'm right), and also wrong. It's true that we can and must identify a culture distinct from Mexico's insofar as the indigenous root is concerned, but we must not forget that Mexican roots spread out and reached its northernmost colony, first through the Tlaxcaltecas who accompanied the early colonists and settled in the barrio, or the *vecindad de Analco,* as they still call it, in the Villa of Santa Fe, precisely where Saint Michael's Chapel stands today.

Later, new shoots appeared with the Vargas Reconquest. Isn't it true that your own family descended from one Juan de Soyago Sosa, a native of Texcoco who accompanied Vargas, together with his future wife, Isabel Cabo Montezuma? Remember how those who accompanied Oñate and then the new settlers who accompanied Vargas are described in the official registers translated in that famous historian's book: a bit of Spanish (the captains, friars, and scribes) and lots of Mexican. In other words, *minha filha,* the waters of the second wave of colonists that arrived upon the shores of the upper Rio Grande in 1692 were already muddy. That is to say that in the veins of these new colonists, many of them recruited from the Valley of Mexico, flowed a blood rendered thick by miscegenation; in some cases by means of almost one and three quarter centuries of *polvitos* between the señoritas of Tenochtitlan, possessors of sweet and seductive *tipilis,* and the "pure blooded" but not very pure gentlemen from Iberia.

Furthermore, our language itself reveals that imported cultural *mestizaje.* Where do you think these linguistically picturesque words come from: tecolote, guajalote, guajolote, coyote, chapopote, camote, elote —no not Mingote, you fool— cuate, chocolate, pichicuate, esquite, mesquite, tequexquite, chíquete, mecate, cajete, zacate, zoquete, jumate, aguacate, cacahuate, nopal, tamal, comal, atole? From various indigenous languages, of course. And then they say that the New Mexican dialect is marked above all by its archaic castillian modalities. Let's take a look, let's do a limited quantitative comparison: asina, mesmo, acual, vido, vide, trujo, truje, trujimos, en pos de, ende, endenantes, naidien, muncho, cuasi, anque, lección, escuro, curre, lamber, jallar, jeder, jondo, juir, jueron, jumadera. Looks like a tie to me. And you hit the bull's eye with that one: mestizaje is a tie of sorts. So if this is indeed the case, I wonder why so much effort has gone into denying one of the primary team players in this match, as has been done so successfully in my homeland?

But don't fool yourself, you're not exactly a *China Poblana*, so don't fill your head with illusions, Pochita. And speaking of illusions, aren't those the outskirts, the suburbs, the squatters' colonies of Mexico City? Blessed be the Lord, I have arrived in the motherland! What do you mean, the motherland? I thought Spain was the true motherland of all *manitos*? Wrong, babe, Spain is my *father*land...

May I help you with your bags, Señorita?

I was looking for Lencho. I wanted to say goodbye to him. Have you seen him?

Listen, Señorita, I know what I'm talking about. For your own good, you'd better not mention that name again. Just forget you ever met that young man.

Mexico, D.F.
16 September, 1972

My dearest Mari,

I stopped by Casa Aztlán and didn't find you, so I must bid you farewell by letter. At this very moment I am at the airport, and in thirty minutes I will be leaving this country for an indefinite period of time. I wish I could tell you where I'm headed, but I'm not sure myself. I can only tell you that last night two of my friends were shot, and by a very small coincidence (what you would call a minor miracle) I was not with them. To remain in Mexico would no doubt cost me my life; thus, I will have to continue my work elsewhere. You know all too well that there is no shortage in this world of *hermanos y hermanas,* hungry for bread and justice.

Mari, I would like more than anything to be with you right now, tomorrow and always. However, there are things in life that we have to do because otherwise our lives would be bereft of meaning. I can't say when I'll be back in Mexico. But by that time, you'll probably already have returned to your land. I hope that somewhere, sometime, we will see each other once again. In the meantime, the dream of a more human world and your precious image will sustain my struggle.

I just remembered, as the wonderful moments we spent together are flashing on the screen of my memory, that I never told you about the scar on my back. Please understand, it still pains me so much to think about that horrible and insane moment, that I can not bring myself to speak of it. I promise, however, that at our next reunion I will tell you all.

A thousand kisses,
Sergio

Sometimes
in my dreams
I'm still riding
that train called absence,
grasping a one-way ticket
tightly
in my hand.

An Alternative Journey: The Complexities of *Paletitas de Guayaba*

by Tey Diana Rebolledo
Distinguished Professor of Spanish
The University of New Mexico

Paletitas de Guayaba by Erlinda Gonzales-Berry was first published in 1991 by a small New Mexican publishing house, Academia/El Norte Publications, which focused on publishing books in Spanish written by New Mexicans. The edition was limited in number and distribution was almost nonexistent. Nevertheless, *Paletitas* was widely read in college classes and by the Hispano community in New Mexico and became a sort of underground classic. It was one of the few Chicano/a novels that was published in Spanish; other writers such as Miguel Méndez *(Peregrinos de Aztlán* 1974*)*, Aristeo Brito (*El diablo en Tejas* 1976), and Margarita Cota-Cárdenas *(Puppet* 1985), Alejandro Morales (*Caras viejas y vino Nuevo)* among others, had also published in Spanish, but they were the exceptions to the rule. Most Chicano/a writers published their work in English with some bilingual code switching or with the occasional Spanish word or phrase.

Actually, *Paletitas de Guayaba* had difficulties finding a publisher. When sent to such Chicano publishing houses as Arte Público Press and Bilingual Review Press, it was pronounced too short because it was only 92 pages long or too didactic because of its political and social commentary. Adding to the difficulty was, of course, the fact that it was written in Spanish. In addition, once it was published and was circulating, an adverse review was published in the *Albuquerque Journal.* In this review, the critic, a student who was a native of Spain, clearly did not understand the book and was not familiar with the avant-guard literary techniques utilized by contemporary Latin American and Chicano/writers. She commented on the difficulty she had reading it, saying "it becomes quite a task to follow the story line when we are constantly jumping from character to author speaking and then to character again" (Clarimón). She did not understand the self referential and auto consciousness nature of the novel nor the irony implicit in it. She also failed to understand the subversions of writing as Gonzales-Berry in liberated-Chicana feminist language by appropriating taboo words traditionally forbidden to women. Moreover, the reviewer was not familiar with Chicano/a literature as a discourse of resistance to the dominant canon, which marginalized it. And so, the *novela* has remained an underground book, made even more so when it quickly went out of print. Now, translated and newly published, this novel should appropriately find its place more prominently in Chicano/a literature.

A native New Mexican, Gonzales-Berry was born in a small ranching community in northern New Mexico in 1942. After finishing her MA and PhD at the University of New Mexico she taught for various years at Earlham College and one year at New Mexico State University. She returned to the University of New Mexico where she became the coordinator of the Heritage Language Program, and later Chair of the Department of Spanish and Portuguese. While there, she was instrumental in establishing the Southwest Studies MA in the Spanish Department. Dr. Erlinda Gonzales-Berry is Professor Emeritus from Oregon State University where she was Chair of the Ethnic Studies Program, and director of Casa Latinos Unidos de Benton County. Gonzales-Berry has been extremely active as a scholar as well as a creative writer.

While at the University of New Mexico, she participated in an informal creative writing atmosphere, which included published and unpublished writers, such as Gustavo Saenz, Sabine Ulibarrí, and Esteban Arrellano. Moreover, the Department had a tradition of supporting creative writers such as Spanish poet Angel González and novelist Alfredo Rodríguez. In addition, Gonzales-Berry wrote her doctoral dissertation on the Chicano narrative, "Chicano Literature in Spanish: Roots and Content," analyzing writers such as

Ulibarrí, Rolando Hinojosa, Sergio Elizondo, Tomás Rivera, Alejandro Morales, Miguel Méndez and Aristeo Brito, all of whom wrote in Spanish. It was in this creative milieu that *Paletitas de Guayaba* was born.

Paletitas de Guayaba is a search and journey toward derstanding the complex nature of identity formation in the mind of the young heroine, Mari. It is a road trip (although mostly by train) to the heart of being a Chicana and toward a transnational identity and what that means in terms of nation, race, gender and sexuality. In the book, Mari travels to Mexico searching for her roots, but finds that, although her family's origins were from Mexico, she is not considered a Mexican by Mexicans. In this bildungsroman or growing up story, she faces various challenges to both her sense of identity and to herself, such as attempted seductions, intellectual and cultural indoctrinations, and "a series of competing notions of what constitutes multiculturalism" (Chabram-Dernersesian, 276). In her analysis of *Paletitas,* Angie Chabram-Dinersesian argues that as Mari attempts to reclaim her past, her identity is "contested at every turn," both by Mexican and Chicano males, who in addition see her as a sex object. For Chabram-Dernersesian the negotiation of Mari's relations and the questioning of their meaning by way of extensive inner monologues and academic definitions of concepts are a "kind of pedagogy of resistance in light of the rampant ignorance about her mode of living out a Chicana/o Mexicana/o transnational experience"277). She also points out that, since Mari is a Chicana relocating herself back to Mexico, the narrative creates a new dialogue of multicultural or transnational difference and sameness that allow Mari to participate in a wider conversation between Chicanas of Mexican descent living in the United States and contemporary Mexicans. Chabram-Dernersesian argues that, in general, the Chicano connection with Mexican ancestry is usually seen from a position of the United States. In the case of *Paletitas,* which takes place during Mari's trip to Mexico, Mari needs to determine her identity in relation to Mexico, and to deal with it on a day to day basis, negotiations, which Chabram says are "often painful, ironic, sarcastic, and humorous... responding to national dynamics, to regional dynamics, to gender dynamics, to racial dynamics, to sexual dynamics and to the politics of the movement. Finally, it means confronting the discourse of the brown female other, the Pochita, at the point of origin" (277).

The original cover of the book is an actual picture of the author with her older sister, dressed for a tourist photograph in *china poblana* costumes: costumes which are the icons of Mexican cultural identity. Because the narrative is a questioning of the meanings of identity, the cover simultaneously reflects dressing up into identity while deconstructing it.[1] While the cover was constructed from a black and white photograph, the artist Soledad Marjon was asked to hand color it, as many photographs of the time were hand tinted. Instead of merely emphasizing a few features in the photograph, as was traditional, Marjon produced a colorful and complex decorative painting which in turn reflects, it seems to me, the complex structure of the novel and the profound issues examined in it.

The book begins on the 12th of December, the feast day and celebration of the Virgen de Guadalupe, Mexico's patron virgin, her national symbol and the first *mestiza* saint, not to say Pocha. It ends on the 16th of September, Mexico's Independence Day celebration. It is clear that in the significant span of nine months the narrative will examine what it is be a Mexican, how much of that identity the heroine can claim, what she can use, and what she will discard.

The structure of the *novela* is a dialogue with Sergio and with the narrator herself. Intermixed is also a letter to a lover, Steve, perhaps never sent, the words of hawkers selling goods on the train, recollections of her family history, a dream sequence (and a footnote explaining the character in the dream, *Doña Marina*), conversations with Lencho, a conductor on the train and others, and finally a letter from Sergio. The conversation with Sergio seems to be one-sided, from Mari's point of view; even though she answers what seem to be questions and observations from Sergio, he never speaks throughout the novel. The auto-consciousness of the narrator breaks through when she directly asks the readers our opinion as to why he does not speak, giving us options to choose. One obvious option is that she has projected him as the ideal male (an ironic commentary since his behavior clearly demonstrates that he is not), but better still that he may be her muse, or her consciousness to whom she is speaking (*Paletitas*, 39). He may also be a revolutionary or a terrorist (it is unclear why he has to leave the country in a hurry), but then he may also be a symbol for what the narration is all about. As I commented in another place, in Mari's discussions with Sergio, "the subject and the object become confused as the subject positions and repositions herself as a thinking, writing, and seeing subject, one who has come to consciousness within and about the sociopolitical text and context "(Rebolledo, 179).

While these conversations may seem like a first person narration from the locus of the narrator, they quickly dissipate into a musing on philosophy and politics from a point of view which shifts and changes as it jumps from the present to the past to the future and assertions and contradictions. It is like being on a train with constantly new vistas clicking by. In addition, we understand that, as she is speaking, she is also writing the novel, so the bildungsroman becomes a künstlerroman, or an account of how the narrator becomes a writer.[2]

The original narrative is beautifully written mainly in Spanish and the language registers flow from a highly articulate use of the Spanish language to a language of popular culture, slang, Caló and bilingualism. The book has short vignettes separated by a mark which separates letters from narration from thoughts from dreams (which also appear in italics), and may seem chaotic to the untrained reader. But clearly the narrative techniques mimic the thought process as well as the oral conversational stream of consciousness style where elements that do not seem central to the conversation are triggered by that very conversation itself.

While the book may seem like a romance, in reality it is anything but. It discusses Mari's relationships with men as both enlightening and threatening, and contains a colloquial language which discusses sexual names and euphemisms in no uncertain terms. As Mari muses on the ability of language to circumvent reality, she also understands that naming sexual parts gives her power. Her subversion of traditional methods of story telling, as well as the often shocking and direct use of language and descriptions take Marina's storytelling beyond her story, "she seizes the language by appropriating male public language and imposing on that language the alterity, or otherness, of speaking the female body, of speaking female sexuality" (Rebolledo 177).

Another noteworthy technique is the use of meta-narrative or allusions or references to other writers as well as *personajes* and historical events which deepen and amplify the complexity of the narrative. One reference in the novel talks about the spread in literature from Hemingway to Woody Allen, from serious novelist to popular culture, all of which are to be found in the narrative. When, later in life, Mari reads over her journal, she realizes there is material for serious writing. Too, there are multiple references to Latin American writers and revolutionaries such as José Agustín, Victor Jara, Che Guevara, Carlos Fuentes and Octavio Paz as well as to Chicana/o writers such as Denise Chávez and Sergio Elizondo. Contemporary and ancient Mexican history also form a background to the novel as seen in the history of the massacre at Tlatelolco and the struggle against colonialism in New Mexico. Morever, there is a dream scene in which Mari speaks directly with *Doña* Marina/La Malinche her namesake, the woman who was taken by Hernán Cortés as a lover and who translated for him during the conquest of Mexico. In this sequence, *Doña* Marina explains her actions, defending herself from the accusations of being a traitor to her country and asserting that she is the creator of a new race of which Mari is the end product.

As mentioned before, the narrative alternates between the journey on the train as Mari travels to Mexico City and the emotional and cultural journey taking place during her stay there. In both journeys she is constantly growing and understanding the challenges she faces until she comes to an understanding as to who she is. While Clarimón stated that Mari does not find personal growth, she could not have been more wrong. It is in the very complex understanding of how to find that third space between the longed-for motherland and tongue (Mexico) and the conflict of her place of birth (the United States), between "serious" writing and popular culture, between "synthesis and syncretism," that "constant

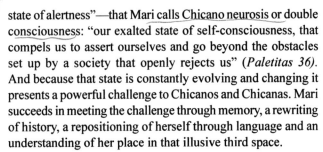

state of alertness"—that Mari calls Chicano neurosis or double consciousness: "our exalted state of self-consciousness, that compels us to assert ourselves and go beyond the obstacles set up by a society that openly rejects us" (*Paletitas 36*). And because that state is constantly evolving and changing it presents a powerful challenge to Chicanos and Chicanas. Mari succeeds in meeting the challenge through memory, a rewriting of history, a repositioning of herself through language and an understanding of her place in that illusive third space.

Paletitas de Guayaba is just that, a delicious piece of fruit ice that tickles your palate, teases your tongue and when you are finished, entices you for more.

Bibliography

Chabram-Dernersesian, "'Chicana! Rican? No, Chicana Riqueña!'" Refashioning the Transnational Connection" in Kaplan, Caren, Norma Alarcón and Minoo Moallem, eds. *Between Woman and Nation. Nationalisms, Transnational Feminisms, and the State.* Durham and London: Duke University Press, 1999, 264-295.

Clarimón, Estefanía, "Long Journey in Few Words," *Albuquerque Journal*, November 19, 1991, G8.

García, Nasario. *Pláticas. Conversations with Hispano Writers of New Mexico.* Lubbock: Texas Tech University Press, 2000.

Rebolledo, Tey Diana. *Women Singing in the Snow.* Tucson: The University of Arizona Press, 1995.

Torres, Héctor. *Conversations with Contemporary Chicana and Chicano Writers.* Albuquerque: University of New Mexico Press, 2007.

Endnotes

1 Similarly in *Canícula* by Norma Cantú, the author uses tourist pictures of herself and of her mother dressed in china poblana outfits to question and undermine the concept of identity and its creation.

2 Many Chicana novels and autobiographies of this period are künstlerromans: such as *Face of an Angel* by Denise Chávez, *Puppet* by Margarita Cota-Cárdenas, and *House on Mango Street* by Sandra Cisneros.

CPSIA information can be obtained at www.ICGtesting.com
Printed in the USA
BVOW05s0013101214

378508BV00001B/40/P

9 781888 205206